Accolades for *Brain Magick*

"All real Magick requires both dedication and skill, here Phil Farber delivers both. This is a guide to tapping into the living magistery of the universe."

—Dr. Richard Bandler,
co-founder of NLP

"Philip Farber is a master magician, and in this scientifically sound, well-researched book he shares a bounty of time-honored alchemical secrets for reinventing reality, as well as personal experiences that shed light on how to best utilize the transformative tools that he provides. For those seeking to shamanically combine the practical and spiritual aspects of their lives, this unique integration of neuroscience, psychology, and ceremonial magick is essential reading."

—David Jay Brown,
coauthor of *Mavericks of the Mind and Conversations on the Edge of the Apocalypse*

"For the scientifically minded, *Brain Magick* is a tour de force of practical exercises backed by solid neuroscience that will change your brain and your magic. Phil Farber breaks down the actual neurological mechanisms of magic so the reader can build their own powerful experiences. Relying on NLP and neuroscience, *Brain Magick* is a unique key to the mystical and magical states alluded to in the body of esoteric knowledge."

—Andrieh Vitimus,
author of *Hands-On Chaos Magic*

"Useful for the beginning mage or the seasoned magician, *Brain Magick* moves from easily understood, easily applied to incredibly complex and in-depth magicks. As usual, Farber's sparkling and whimsical wit seasons this very serious work of artful technology. Farber's mastery of both magickal technology and neuro-linguistic programming come together to create a work destined to become a well-worn tome in any serious magician's collection.

—LaSara Firefox Allen,
MPNLP, author, and coach

"Phil Farber captures the very essence of magickal training and offers a concise series of exercises designed to develop the magickal mind, the will, and the true self. Students of the esoteric arts will find this to be a veritable goldmine of techniques and explanations providing a practical toolkit for exploration of those hidden realms referred to as 'occult.' Without doubt, Phil Farber is a major force in modern magickal thinking and practice today."

—Andrew T. Austin, author of
The Rainbow Machine: Tales from a Neurolinguist's Journal

To Atem: We give you attention, language,
passion, fitting, trance, and making.
You give us the gods.

Brain Magick

About the Author

Philip H. Farber (New York's Hudson Valley) is a respected author and magician who teaches at Maybe Logic Academy. A certified hypnotist, hypnotist instructor, and licensed NLP trainer, Farber has written three books on magick. Visit him online at Meta-Magick.com.

To Write to the Author

If you wish to contact the author or would like more information about this book, please write to the author in care of Llewellyn Worldwide, and we will forward your request. Both the author and publisher appreciate hearing from you and learning of your enjoyment of this book and how it has helped you. Llewellyn Worldwide cannot guarantee that every letter written to the author can be answered, but all will be forwarded. Please write to:

Philip H. Farber
℅ Llewellyn Worldwide
2143 Wooddale Drive
Woodbury, MN 55125-2989

Please enclose a self-addressed stamped envelope for reply, or $1.00 to cover costs. If outside the USA, enclose an international postal reply coupon.

Brain Magick

exercises in meta-magick and invocation

Philip H. Farber

Llewellyn Publications
Woodbury, Minnesota

FIRST EDITION
First Printing, 2011

Book design by Bob Gaul
Cover art © Neuron: iStockphoto.com/Sebastian Kaulitzki,
Ancient Script: iStockphoto.com/Christian Misje
Cover design by Ellen Lawson
Editing by Ed Day

Library of Congress Cataloging-in-Publication Data
Farber, Philip H.
Brain magick : exercises in meta-magick and invocation / Philip H. Farber. — 1st ed.
p. cm.
Includes bibliographical references and index.
ISBN 978-0-7387-2926-8
1. Magic. 2. Invocation. 3. Consciousness—Miscellanea. I. Title.
BF1621.F35 2011
133.4'3—dc23
2011022293

Llewellyn Publications
A Division of Llewellyn Worldwide Ltd.
2143 Wooddale Drive
Woodbury, MN 55125-2989
www.llewellyn.com

Printed in the United States of America

Contents

Exercises

INTRODUCTION

The Way of Woohoo

Consider the possibility of a full-sensory story, something like a motion picture, only more so, or like virtual reality, only even richer in information. The story is created from real perception—things that you can see, hear, touch, taste, and smell. Perceptions and states of consciousness flow into a kind of narrative, not necessarily in a straight line, more a sort of cloud or swarm, vaguely organized—though not always—along an axis of time. Even in that disorganization, the flow of attention, the part of the plot we follow through the swarm, may zig and zag from any perception to almost any other, the entirety of the story only becoming clear after we have partaken of thousands and thousands of memories, feelings, and experiences.

It's the ultimate medium: a palette of every color, sound, feeling, scent, and flavor. It can be populated with multitudes of characters—family, friends, lovers, teachers, neighbors, strangers, good guys, bad guys, heroes, schmucks, and everyone else. It can be beautifully simple or complex beyond the rendering of any supercomputer.

If you were the author of this amazing, full-sensory story, think about the kinds of choices you could make. When the plot arc, the scope of the tale, finally rises into view, just what kind of story do you hope it will be?

There are billions of people with access to this exciting medium—but only some of them even realize that they are the authors, the directors, and the producers of their own full-sensory story. Shakespeare told us that we are but players; what he failed to mention is that, like him, we can also turn the tale toward our own aesthetic ends. Of the few humans who even think about their world enough to realize their own artistic control, only a few have figured out the techniques. The result is that many of the full-sensory stories out there—billions of them—really suck. Or, for the most part, they are repetitive, predictable, and unremarkable lives based around B-movie (or worse!) plots.

The question then becomes—how much do you want your own story to really rock? How exquisite, grand, powerful, intriguing, seductive, exciting, or mythic would you like your experience to be? What excites your neurons, strokes your sense of aesthetics, fulfills your philosophy, applies significance to your circumstance, or makes you scream and shout? Whatever it is that puts the sauce on the omelet, the brushstroke to the *Starry Night,* the bubbles in the Jacuzzi, the ecstasy in viewing a blue arc of summer sky, we shall refer to here as *woohoo.*

Woohoo is the subtle difference between ordinary and exciting, the factor that makes just another stranger into your friend, your teacher, or your lover. Woohoo is what turns an activity into a passion; it's what changes noise into song, foot movement into dance, travel into adventure, procreation into eros, and biological processes into a life worth living. Woohoo is the measure of intensity. It's what continues to draw your attention, moment after moment. It's what makes a feeling worth having. Like the Tao, true woohoo has no definite form. Your personal way of woohoo cannot be named; it is a flow of experience that changes from moment to moment.

Woohoo can be thought of as more of a *how* than a *what*. A camera angle may make the difference between a home video and awe-inspiring cinematography. A nuance of pitch or timbre might separate a technically correct piano recital from a heartfelt virtuoso performance. Duration and subtlety of movement might make the difference between a goodnight kiss and an exciting erotic invitation. How we perceive may determine the quality of woohoo as much as what we perceive the content of that experience. The way that we process our sensory input includes, somewhere along the way, the decision to put our inner artist to work, for our brains to portray our experience with the right camera angle, the sweetest emphasis of tone, or with erotic subtlety. That decision, to woohoo or not to woohoo, usually happens outside of our conscious awareness. We can, however, make it a conscious choice.

The pursuit of a woohoo-filled life story, whatever the details of that might be for you, is the *Way of Woohoo*.

The Model of Meta-Magick

Magick, as we're using the term here, refers to a means of first perfecting the self so that the things that one may do will be done with power and effectiveness. This has always been the aim of magick—to understand the relationship between consciousness and the world in a way that allows us to re-create ourselves (and our world) in hedonic, healthy, and practical ways. Our understanding and self-perfection allow us to fit into the world so well that we can influence it in accordance with our will.

Meta-Magick is a collection of opportunities to think about magick. Elements from a variety of theories and models, ranging from neuroscience to voodoo, are offered as clues to understand the phenomena we find in our magical experiments. There are many different styles and practices of magick, in every culture, on every continent. By identifying some of the common elements, we are better able to separate out the magick itself, the techniques and practices that really work, from the content of the rituals that relates to specific belief systems. In general, many techniques of magick are the same everywhere, with their intent aimed at different results and deities. This suggests that the rituals and practices derive from the commonality of human experience; this is how our brains work when we do magick.

Our focus will be on the magical operation of invocation. If you are already familiar with magick and invocation techniques, you may be able to use the exercises in this book to identify the behaviors and experiences that make those techniques effective for you. If you are completely new to these concepts (relax, all will be explained soon.), you can use the methods given here as building blocks for your own techniques and magical rituals.

We'll start with a premise that magick is, at least in one important way, like every other human behavior: it derives from the interplay of our mind/body and the world. Anything that we can do, magically or otherwise, will be represented by corresponding processes in our brains, our bodies, and our behavior. While that may not be all that happens, it offers us important clues to how we can replicate magical results and utilize the tools that we have—our perceptions and abilities.

Two questions to keep in mind while experimenting with this book are: "Which of my behaviors contribute to making magick?" and "How can I use those behaviors to create maximum woohoo in my life?"

Experimental results will undoubtedly differ from person to person. Ultimately, the model of magick and the direction that you take toward increased woohoo can be unique to you. There are no right or wrong results for any of the experiments. Whatever happens becomes data for your own map to the realm of woohoo. In short, this is magick about magick, rituals and techniques designed to help us understand more about rituals and magical techniques. When we begin to work with others and compare results, we may be able to create more generalized models of magick.

Meta-Magick exercises can be practiced as a separate system of magick; however, it is just as interesting to apply the insights gained from this exploration to a practice or system you may already be familiar with. Or use these techniques to develop your own, personal system of magick from scratch. Or find the woohoo wherever it may lie and gather it into everything you see, hear, feel, taste, and smell throughout your life. In short, use this book to bring some woohoo to whatever you do.

The Model of Science

Think of science, like Meta-Magick, as a means for creating models. An all-too-common perception of science is that it deals in authoritative facts—truths that are immutably recorded in peer-reviewed journals and blessed by academia. In actuality, science is a method of inquiry that generates theories. Theories are forms of metaphor that explain a body of data, although scientists often may shy away from admitting the metaphoric quality. Metaphors are rarely perfect and almost always leave a lot of room for interpretation. Theories are updated, hopefully on a regular basis, to best fit the map of the world we operate from.

The bits and pieces of neuroscience that illustrate the ideas in this book are by no means definitive—and it is likely that my interpretation of those bits and pieces may be quite different from that of the scientists who proposed them. As this is a book about the magical art of invocation, not neuroscience, we will explore only a tiny portion of the huge and complex subject of the human brain. This is done as a way of building operating metaphors and not, by any means, a complete or necessarily "true" map of neurological functions. These theories can help develop the hypotheses that we use to initiate our experiments and, as "operating metaphors," they help build a frame through which to view and understand our responses.

The more important parts of this book, the exercises, provide a framework for creating experiments. Consider your explorations of woohoo as a process of personal scientific inquiry, with your own consciousness as laboratory. For those not already familiar with scientific method, the steps are fairly simple:

1. The scientist creates a hypothesis. A hypothesis is an educated guess at an outcome that we can test with an experiment. For instance, "If I read this book and practice the exercises, I'll learn something about magick and the brain."
2. An experiment is designed to test the hypothesis. In this case, the experiment might be actually reading the book and practicing the exercises, and then testing your knowledge of magick against what it was prior to reading and practicing.
3. After repeated experiments—perhaps involving other people reading and practicing, or perhaps reading and practicing from other magick books—a theory can be formed. The theory might be a denial or confirmation of the hypothesis, or it might be something else entirely, deduced from the experience.

In short, I hope that you will be scientific in this personal way, that you will perform the experiments and eventually, when you think you have enough data, draw your own conclusions about the processes of invocation and the nature of woohoo.

Do the experiments and draw your own conclusions.

one

States of Consciousness

The Nature of a State

Consciousness flows, ever-changing, from one moment to the next. However minutely or broadly, each nanosecond of experience differs from the preceding one. When we talk about a "state of consciousness," we make a generalization about a collection of such moments, that some aspects of consciousness remain constant, or at least similar, for a period of time. Even so, sensory experience continues its kaleidoscopic change. When we meditate, we ease into a session, first getting comfortable in our posture, then getting into the flow of meditation, then easing back out, aware of comfort or discomfort in our bodies, and turning our attention back outward. Rather than a singular state called "meditation," we may find a continually shifting experience—a process rather than a thing. A hypnotic trance induction has a beginning, middle, and end. A psychedelic experience rises and falls as chemical levels in the bloodstream peak and diminish. Sleep is characterized by several stages through the night.

Knowledge of how we get into and out of different states of consciousness can be incredibly useful in the practice of magick. Some rituals require that the magician be in a particular state prior to beginning. Some rituals—particularly rituals of invocation—are all about inducing powerful altered states. It can be very important for a magician to be able to know when he or she is in a state, when the state is reaching its peak, and when it might be fading. In general, we usually are not aware of the process by which we change and enter states. Think about the last time you were happy—you may remember the content of the experience, the stimuli that pushed you in that direction, but, unless you've played with these kinds of calibration techniques before, the actual feeling of the state coming on and building likely occurred on an unconscious level. That is, you might remember the wonderful present that someone gave you and how happy that made you, but perhaps not the actual process of exactly how it changed you. Similarly, in magical practices we may work hard to remember the words and symbols of a ritual while the process of the experience slips past our awareness. It's okay. It's a normal experience. Now, let's find out how we can bring state changes into conscious awareness.

The nature of a state may best be understood by paying attention to the differences between one state and the next, and the differences from one moment to the next.

To notice a difference, we first have to calibrate, to notice where and what we are now. The simplest method is to ask, "What am I experiencing now?"

Exercise 1.1 Physiological Calibration

To begin, find out how your body is functioning right now. Run through each of the physiology questions and answer them to the best of your ability.

Physiology

- What is the position of my body?
- Am I moving or still? How so?
- What are the positions of my arms, legs, hands, and feet?
- Is my heartbeat in my conscious awareness? If so, is it fast or slow, strong or weak?
- Is my breathing rapid, slow, even, uneven, shallow, or deep?
- Am I breathing from the upper part, middle, or bottom of my lungs?
- Which of my muscles are in use? Which are relaxed? How in use or relaxed are they?

Once you have determined the answers to these questions, you can change your state using Expansion and Contraction Breathing and run through the physiology modeling questions again, noting any changes that have occurred.

- **Expansion and Contraction Breathing**— at least five minutes: Imagine a circle around yourself, at about the diameter of your outspread arms. Sit or stand in the center of that circle. Fill your lungs completely, with a slow, even inhalation. As you inhale, allow your attention to expand to fill the circle. As you exhale, slowly, evenly, and completely, allow your attention to contract to a single point in the center of your chest. Repeat.

How have the physical parameters of your state changed? Has your position changed? Or your heartbeat, breathing, and musculature?

Modeling Resources

We can be more precise in modeling states by identifying and measuring a variety of perceptions, behaviors, and beliefs that can help us to define the processes we refer to as states. Here are some more **Modeling Resources** that can be applied to states of every kind.

Sensory-Based Model

In the model of perception and behavior used in the field of Neuro-Linguistic Programming (NLP), thought and experience are sorted and represented through "sensory representational systems," visual, auditory, kinesthetic, olfactory, and gustatory—seeing, hearing, feeling, smelling, and tasting. These are not only the senses that we use to experience in the present; they are also the ways that we sort our thoughts and memories internally. A **sensory-based model** can give us some idea of what and, even better, how we are using our senses while in a particular state of consciousness. Reflect on the following questions.

- Am I aware more externally or internally?
- How much am I consciously aware in visual mode?
- Do the things I see (with eyes open or closed) seem bright, dim, colorful, distant, close, large, small, shiny, dull, etc.?
- How much am I consciously aware in auditory mode?
- Do the things I hear sound loud, quiet, tonal, rhythmic, vocal, deep, high, distant, close, distinct, fuzzy, etc.?
- How much am I consciously aware in kinesthetic mode?
- Do the things I feel seem tactile, visceral, emotional, proprioceptive, mild, intense, large, small, tingly, pressing, moving, still, warm, cold, etc.?
- How much am I consciously aware in olfactory and gustatory modes?
- Do the things I taste and smell seem intense, mild, pungent, sweet, smoky, musky, fruity, sour, bitter, spicy, etc.?
- Is it easy or difficult to separate one sense from another?
- Are senses represented to consciousness as other senses, that is, sound experienced as color, color experienced as feeling, and so on?

- Am I experiencing from my own point of view, or seeing/hearing/feeling myself as if from someone else's point of view?
- How much am I concerned with how I feel about my sensory experiences?

After calibrating and testing an altered state, what differences did you find? Which senses characterized your baseline state and which were you using during your altered state?

Eight Circuit Brain Model

The model of an **Eight Circuit Brain** was originally proposed by Timothy Leary as a way of sorting behavioral tendencies, imprints, "life scripts," and "reality tunnels," among other uses. The model was further expanded on by other writers and thinkers, including Robert Anton Wilson and Antero Alli. The following modeling questions are based on Wilson's explanations of the model.

Am I processing my sensory information via Circuit One:

- Am I motivated to move toward comfort and/or away from discomfort?
- Am I motivated toward food and drink?

Am I processing my sensory information via Circuit Two:

- Am I concerned about my importance relative to other people?
- Do I want to fight or run away?

- Is my behavior expressed as dominance or submission?

Am I processing my sensory information via Circuit Three:

- Am I thinking about things more than doing them?
- Am I motivated by logic, intellectual curiosity, or scientific interest?
- Am I talking a lot? Or talking to myself in my head?

Am I processing my sensory information via Circuit Four:

- Am I concerned or motivated by my family or sexual relationships?
- Am I horny?
- Am I motivated by the way I appear to others, in regard to my masculinity, femininity, or androgeny?

Am I processing my sensory information via Circuit Five:

- Do I experience movement of "energy," "light," "vibration," or temperature in or near my body?
- Am I easily able to control my rate of breathing, heart rate, and comfort level?
- Do I feel "high," "stoned," "trippy," "floating," or otherwise positively experiencing a body/mind-based, sensory experience?

Am I processing my sensory information via Circuit Six:

- Do I recognize the experience I'm having as "magick" or "brain-change?"
- Am I acutely aware of the social/cultural programming of myself or of others around me?
- Does human behavior seem like an abstract concept based on arbitrary, random, and easily altered rules?
- Am I aware of choices to alter, abolish, or create forms of my own inner programming?

Am I processing my sensory information via Circuit Seven:

- Am I conscious of experiences in terms of "past lives," "future memories," or "magical currents?"
- Am I aware of the interconnectedness of things?
- Do ordinary things seemed imbued with symbolic meaning?
- Am I aware of or motivated by an evolutionary concern?

Am I processing my sensory information via Circuit Eight:

- Can my experience be described as "out of body," "lucid dreaming," "bilocation," or " astral projection?"
- Does reality itself seem like an abstract concept based on arbitrary, random, and easily altered presuppositions? ("There is no spoon.")

- Do concepts such as location, size, direction, time, and so forth seem meaningless, arbitrary, or laughable?
- Do I experience my universe as a singularity?[1]

What was the difference in experience between your calibrated baseline state and your altered state? Which circuits were characteristic of each state?

NLP Meta-Programs Model

Richard Bandler, one of the cofounders of NLP, originally suggested the idea of **meta-programs** as patterns of behavior that help us to organize other behaviors. Meta-programs help describe our general approach in a situation rather than the specifics of our perception and action. It is possible for us to organize our behavior using different, overarching patterns in different states. Meta-programs have been further explored and developed by other NLP practitioners, including Leslie Cameron-Bandler and Robert Dilts. The following questions represent a very simplified version of the model, sufficient for basic state-modeling purposes.

- Are my behaviors motivated away from discomfort or toward pleasure?
- Are my behaviors motivated from my own internal decisions or based on the decisions of others?
- Is my attention more on myself or on others?

- Am I more concerned with generalities or details? The big picture or the individual brushstroke?
- Is my attention directed toward past, present, or future?
- Am I thinking in a long time frame or a short one?
- Am I thinking about how things are alike? Or how things are different?

How did your general tendencies change from your baseline state to your altered state? What meta-programs were characteristic of each state?

Meta-Magick Energy Flow Model

The **Energy Flow Model** found its original inspiration in NLP techniques to access kinesthetic states, described by Richard Bandler, and Steve and Connierae Andreas. This is a very streamlined version, again sufficient for our present purpose. We will explore this technique quite a bit more, later in the book.

Track the kinesthetics of the experience as follows:

- Notice where in your body the feeling of the state begins.
- Notice where it moves to as the experience develops toward its peak.
- Pay attention to whether the feeling is moving or static, cycling or pulsing.
- Give the feeling a color. "If this feeling had a color, what would it be?"

- Experiment by making the colored shape brighter, darker, richer, faded, larger, or smaller to determine which of these increases the feeling associated with the state.
- Notice any other changes in feeling as well as in what you might see, hear, taste, or smell.

What were the differences between your baseline energy flow and your altered state energy flow? What changes in colors, shapes and sizes could you perceive??"

Exercise 1.2 Calibrate, State, Model, Repeat

The techniques for altering consciousness listed below range from simple to moderately complex. Play with as many of these techniques as you comfortably can and attempt to quantify them according to the modeling resources. Remember that the point of the exercises is not necessarily to learn as many altered states techniques as possible, but to learn how to model and understand what our minds and bodies do as we explore different states.

Here's how it goes:

Calibrate, State, Model, Repeat

1. **Calibrate your present state.** Run through the modeling resource categories and questions and mark down the answers, simply and briefly. Use as many of these resources as you think appropriate for each task. It's like filling out a questionnaire—make a list of your responses to each question that seems to apply. Skip any that do not apply

to your particular experience. For now, forget about what any of it means. In fact, at this point it is just raw data, until we have something different to compare it to.

2. **Enter into an altered state** via one of the methods listed below. Enjoy it for as long as you'd like.
3. Then, immediately upon returning (or while remaining as much as possible in the state), **use the modeling resources to build a model of the state.** Use as many of these resources as you think appropriate for each task. Skip any that do not apply to your particular experience.
4. **Repeat** using a different technique to alter your consciousness. It's not necessary to explore all of the methods given, just the few that might draw your interest. You can also use the modeling process with other techniques that you might be familiar with, along with those included here.

Database of Techniques

- **Simple Zen**—at least ten minutes: Sit in a position with your spine vertical and straight (a chair will do nicely). Allow your breathing to become relaxed and natural. Let it set its own rhythm and depth, however it is comfortable. Focus your attention on your breathing, on the movements of your chest and abdomen rather than on your nose and mouth. Keep your attention focused on your breathing. For some people an additional level of concentration may be helpful. You might add a simple counting rhythm, spoken in your head as you breathe: "One" on the inhale, "Two" on the exhale, and repeat. Or you might visualize your breath as a swinging door, swinging in on the inhale and out on the exhale.

- **Ajna Monkey**—at least one hour, days if you can manage it: The following method was suggested by Aleister Crowley in *Magick in Theory and Practice*. One imagines that all your perceptions and thoughts go to or arise from the Ajna chakra, the "third eye" located above the bridge of the nose, between the eyes. Begin by breathing deeply and fully, imagining that you send the breath to the Ajna, not to the lungs. Walk slowly and observe the movements of your legs. Reflect that the legs work because they are guided by nerve impulses from the brain, controlled by the Ajna. "The legs are automatic, like those of a wooden monkey: the power in Ajna is that which does the work, is that which walks. This is not hard to realise, and should be grasped firmly, ignoring all other walking sensations. Apply this method to every other muscular movement . . . Transfer all bodily sensations to the Ajna, e.g., 'I am cold' should mean 'I feel cold,' or better still, 'I am aware of a sensation of cold'—transfer this to the Ajna, 'the Ajna is aware,' etc. . . . Finally, strive hard to drive anger and other obsessing thoughts into the Ajna. Develop a tendency to think hard of

Ajna when these thoughts attack the mind, and let Ajna conquer them. Beware of thinking of 'My Ajna.' In these meditations and practices, Ajna does not belong to you; Ajna is the master and worker, you are the wooden monkey."—Aleister Crowley[2]

- **Chasing the Tail**—at least ten minutes: Chasing the Tail is a simple meditation of self-observation. Sit quietly and pay attention to where your thoughts arise. When you think something—anything—the thoughts appear to come from a particular location in space, usually somewhere in your head or somewhere in your body, although occasionally a thought may seem to arise outside the physical body. Just note where the thought arises and let all other thoughts fall from your mind. As each new thought arises, just note where it comes from. If you have thoughts about the practice itself, note where they come from. If you have thoughts about noting where a thought came from, note where that thought came from. Got it? Like a cat chasing its own tail, you turn your consciousness back on itself.
- **The Betty Erickson Self-Hypnosis Method**—at least five minutes: Sitting comfortably, with eyes open or closed, list (to yourself) three things that you can see, then three things you can hear, then three things you can feel. (For example, "I see the color of the wall, I see the person opposite me, I see the color of her hair, I hear the sounds outside the room, I hear people moving about, I hear my own

breathing, I feel the cushion underneath me, I feel the air on my skin, I feel my hands on my lap ..."). Then narrow it down to a list of two things in each sensory mode, then one thing in each mode. Tell yourself, "As I count from ten down to one, I can go into a deep, comfortable trance." Then count breaths backwards from ten to one and enjoy the trance that you are drifting into. This works most powerfully when the verbal listing within your head is timed in a rhythm with your breathing.

- **Lucid Dreaming**: Lucid dreaming begins when you become aware, while dreaming, that you are, in fact, asleep and dreaming. Once you are aware that it is a dream, you can consciously take the experience in any direction. As an example of how we can work with dream states, consider this basic and effective method for lucid dreaming. Throughout the day, at least a dozen times during the day, test to find out whether or not you are dreaming. For instance, try to fly—if you are in a lucid dream, flying is easy—or read something, look away, then look back and read it again (in dreams, things rarely read the same way twice). There are many other such tests. If you get in the habit of doing this frequently, it carries over into your dream states and then, suddenly, the tests are positive and you are lucid dreaming. This is a popular and effective method used by dreamers all over the world. Along with other "pleasant dreaming" practices (for example, sleep late and when you wake in the morning, stay in exactly the same position and drift off again, wake under your own power, with no alarms, etc.), this will eventually induce lucid dreaming in most people, usually within a week or so.[3]

- **Yogic Breath**—at least ten minutes: Your lungs have three main areas: the bottom, which is controlled by movements of the diaphragm and is visible as a rising and falling of the abdomen ("abdominal breathing"); the middle, controlled by expansion and contraction of the rib cage; and the top, controlled by rising and falling of the shoulder blades. Each of these different kinds of breathing are associated with different states of consciousness. For purposes of the Yogic Breath, however, the key is simply to fill and empty all three of the areas of the lungs. Fill and empty your lungs completely but smoothly, without halting or straining. This is not hyperventilation—it is proper and full breathing, at a relaxed pace.
- **Pranayama—Square Breathing**—at least ten minutes: Once you are comfortable with the Yogic Breath, you can begin to slow it down a bit. Figure out your usual time for an exhalation or inhalation, then add one second to it. Let's say that you normally exhale a Yogic Breath for four seconds—you can now begin to practice pranayama by inhaling for five seconds, holding your breath in for five seconds, then exhaling for five seconds and holding your breath out for five seconds. Five in, five hold, five out, five hold—and repeat.

- **Pranayama—Circular Breathing**—at least ten minutes: Take full, even, Yogic Breaths and entirely eliminate the pauses at the top and bottom of the breath so that your breathing cycle becomes a seamless and constant ebb and flow.
- **The Freedom Dance**—at least twenty minutes: Pick out some great music with a good tempo and dance to it. Get wild. "Dance as if no one is watching." Move freely. Work and play with all your muscles and joints. Explore your range of movement in every limb. Some people are more flexible than others; some have limitations due to injury or illness. Just do as much as you can. Repeat regularly.
- **The Bee Breath**—Begin with a long, slow, full inhalation through both nostrils. Fill your lungs without straining. As you exhale completely and easily through both nostrils, let your throat make a soft "eeee" sound. Five to ten repetitions of this may be enough to notice a change in consciousness. Five to ten minutes is an even better starting place.
- **Mindfulness Meditation**—at least ten minutes: Sit and pay attention to your posture, your breathing and your environment. As thoughts arise in your mind, note them, give them a label, and then let them go. Label them without being judgmental. That is, note that "this is a thought about an itch" … then let it go. Or "this is an emotional thought of love (hate, anxiety, compassion, happiness, etc.)" and then let it go and return your attention to your present experience.

- **Ecstatic Breathing**:
  1. Breathe through your mouth, slowly and evenly, for about one minute.
  2. Breathe by drawing the air into the bottommost part of your lungs, deep into your belly. Start with a slow, even pace, then gradually increase the rate until, finally, you are panting, but still filling and emptying the deepest part of your lungs.
  3. Continue to pant for half a minute then take a deep, full breath, filling your lungs from top to bottom. Hold the breath for ten seconds, then release and breathe slowly and deeply a few times. Then return to panting and repeat this cycle until you have deepened your trance state.
- **Orgasm**—as long as possible: Do I really have to tell you how to do this one?
- **Psychoactive Substances**—Any change in state can be modeled to some extent, and that includes the great diversity of states that can be experienced by allowing our neurology to interact with psychoactive substances. Research the substance you intend to model so that you understand about appropriate dosages, set and setting.

Moving and Breathing

As you explore the process of modeling states (Do it now if you haven't already!), notice in particular the relationship between state and physiology. What you do physically—breathing and moving—affects your state; and your state—meditating, concentrating, etc.—may change your depth or rate of breathing, muscular tension and relaxation, heart rate, and other physiological factors.

The scientific evidence for this two-way street of mind/body influence continues to mount. A recent study demonstrated a correlation between posture and hormone levels. In the study, subjects were asked to adopt "open, expansive postures" or "closed, contractive postures." Hormone levels were tested before and after the postures. Those who briefly adopted the open postures—often a display of dominance in mammals—demonstrated a sudden increase in testosterone and a decrease in cortisol. They felt powerful and relaxed. Those who adopted the closed postures—often a sign of submission in mammals—had exactly the opposite hormonal response. The same results were obtained from both men and women.[4]

Moving

We all have collections of postures and movements that are habitual to us. Some people have very free-flowing movements, others are rigid. Some move quickly, some slowly. Some stretch and some contract. Our bodies are capable of moving in ways that we rarely explore. How often do you raise your arms over your head? Or bend from the hip? Or walk backwards? Or do a cartwheel?

Humans learn to move, when we are small, by watching others and then experimenting until we can imitate the movement. As a result of this process of imitative learning, our habitual movements are often culturally transmitted. This can be fairly obvious when we consider behaviors including gestures, greetings, and social formalities. Cultural ideas of dress and propriety also influence habitual movement. Some clothing is restrictive, for example. A businessman in a tucked-in dress shirt will be unlikely to raise his arms over his head. Women in dresses and skirts learn to cross legs or keep thighs closed to accommodate both dress and propriety. Business footwear is unsuitable for running or climbing. And so on.

Body position and movement are closely associated with states of consciousness. *Not only do posture and motion reflect internal experience, they also influence your state of mind. That you are capable of movement beyond your habitual restrictions suggests states of consciousness that remain latent. These states are there as possibilities only, most of the time. They represent aspects of your unconscious mind, something that remains a part of you but is rarely explored. Your potential.*

That potential, of course, can take many different forms. If you are going to explore movements and combinations of movements that are part of this set of unexplored potential, then by all means **select those that represent exhilarating and motivating experiences.**

Breathing

Breathing, like movement, provides a link to the unconscious mind. The control of breathing is usually outside our awareness, something that just happens while our attention is engaged elsewhere. But we can, at will, change the way we breathe.

Breathing is a vital function upon which most other physiological functions depend. Subtle changes in the depth,

> *frequency or manner of your breathing will induce pervasive change throughout your body. Every organ may be affected in some way, including your heart and your brain.* ***Your state of consciousness is deeply dependent on your breathing.***
>
> *Just as with movement, we have habitual patterns of breathing that we have learned largely from the people around us. We've learned these habits usually on an entirely unconscious level. When we begin to consciously direct our breathing we take conscious control of our state of mind.*—The Book of Exhilaration and Mastery[5]

State Dependency

One way in which we naturally delineate or define states happens through "state dependency" phenomena. When we are in one state of consciousness, it becomes very easy to recall the details of other times, in the past, when we were in a similar state—but much more difficult to remember the sensory details of memories that involve different states.[6]

Ever wander into your kitchen and have to think for a moment to remember just why in hell you came there in the first place? It's a common type of experience and usually not a sign of dementia but, rather, a demonstration of state-dependent memory in action. Let's say that prior to your trip to the kitchen you were watching TV or engrossed in work. When you stood up to go to the kitchen, your physiology changed in a number of ways—standing changes blood pressure, heart rate, proprioception, breathing, muscle use, and more. Perhaps the environment you were vegging out or working in was dim and quiet and the kitchen brighter and noisier. In short, you not only walked into a different room, but a different state as well. In the "kitchen state," it's tough to recall what you were thinking about in the "vegging out" state. Fun, huh? It's also an important clue to the nature of woohoo, and perhaps to the whereabouts of your lost car keys.

As far back as the 1940s, research was undertaken in which students studied while under the influence of various drugs and then, later, were tested on the study material. These experiments found that students who were slightly drunk when they studied did better on tests when they were, again, slightly drunk. Students who hit the books while buzzed, however, did less well on tests when they were sober. A few cups of coffee would help students stay alert and awake while studying, but unfortunately, unless they had a similar quantity of caffeine in their system at test-time, it didn't seem to help their memory. Drunk and caffeinated students perpetuate this information about state-dependent learning as if it were an urban legend—and yet the research, if any of us can remember properly, is real.[7]

Likewise, people who are depressed often find it easy to remember every other time in their lives when things sucked. And people who are happy have easy access to all the memories proving what a wonderful life they have. The more common forms of amnesia are often the work of state-dependent memory—suddenly finding yourself home after a long drive, wondering how you got there; or the kind of memory black-outs that happen after serious over-imbibing, serious head injuries, or even every night from a less-serious good night's sleep.

State-dependent memory may be one very good reason why magick students are frequently exhorted to write down their experiences and to keep good records of their experiments—

sometimes important information can be forgotten when we step out of the context and state of the ritual.

Sleep and dreaming are among the more notable states of consciousness that everyone experiences, so our time with the sandman allows for interesting opportunities to explore state-related phenomena.

Exercise 1.3 Dreams and State Dependency

Make a practice, over at least a few days, of taking a moment after you wake up in the morning to **remember any dreams you may have had.** Take that moment whether or not you immediately remember a dream. Attempt this experiment in two different ways: 1. **Sit up** immediately upon waking and attempt to recall your dreams. 2. **Stay in exactly the same position** you find yourself upon waking, without moving a muscle, and attempt to recall your dreams. Which way do you find more successful?

Knowing how our minds access memory through state dependency may prove continually useful throughout our exploration of woohoo. For now, let's highlight a few important concepts:

- **If each state has a particular database of information available to it, then each new state we explore can be a revelation of previously hidden or occult information.**
- **Only by experiencing, over time, our natural range of states can we have access to all our own knowledge, skills, and possibilities.**

- **The abilities necessary to select, establish, re-access, and modify states are essential tools of the woohoologist.**

It's the third point that concerns us now. If our different states are the repositories of different skills and information, being able to re-access those states at will can assure that we have the right skills and information at the right time. Sometimes it's very easy. A variety of sensory cues can trigger the onset of states. Thinking about the punch line of a joke might re-access a chuckle. Remembering the particular touch or sigh or sight of an erotic experience can return you to a state of arousal. The first taste of a morning cup of coffee might elicit a state of stimulation long before the caffeine has time to work. But sometimes it's not so easy. Being asked to recall even familiar information "under pressure," that is, in a more stressful state than usual, can be tricky. It can be difficult to remember the lyrics or melody of a song while listening to another song or moving to a different rhythm. And for some people, trying to remember a person's name when you meet them in an unexpected context might be a challenge or even embarrassing. This kind of experience will be different for every person, but we all bump against the limits of our states from time to time.

Natural Anchors

The ability to remember and draw upon any experience at any time—to transcend the boundaries that separate our state-dependent selves and tap into those states that carry important information, skills, and feeling—can be very useful. The simplest method for accessing states uses the natural sensory cues that we associate with the experiences. The tone of a lover's voice, the face of a friend, the smell of a particular spice or incense, the feel of a particular chair, or a few words from a favorite poem or book can all elicit states. These are called *anchors* and are multifarious and diverse. Anchors are sensory cues that are associated with a particular response. On the simplest level, an anchor is like the sound of the bell that drove Pavlov's dog into a state of salivating hunger. Anchors can be created for humans just like ringing a bell—and we'll create some intentional anchors a bit further into our exploration of woohoo—but for now let's examine the anchors that are already there, that are created as an inevitable part of every sensory experience.

Anchors are an essential component in posthypnotic response. The classic idea of the posthypnotic response involves a key word that, when uttered, will trigger a particular reaction or re-access a trance state. The hypnotist Milton Erickson noticed that when a memory or action was recovered using an anchor, subjects would also experience a return to the state they were in when the memory or action first occurred. These trance states could be prolonged or they might be fleeting, momentary shifts of consciousness. With this in mind, both natural and intentional anchors can be understood as important tools to access memories and the associated states.

The part of an experience that can best be used as an anchor will, like most of the experiences we are discussing here, vary widely from person to person. If three people go to a concert and all are transported to states of musical ecstasy, the sensory cue that later pulls one back into an ecstatic memory might be the rhythm; for another it might be the lights; and for the third it might be the lyrics that rekindles the reverie. If you already know the anchors that can recall a memory, begin there. If specific anchors are not yet known, a basic method is simply to run through perceptual details in all of the senses.

Take a few moments now, with the following exercise, to identify some of your own naturally occurring anchors.

Exercise 1.4 Hypnotic Memories

- **Identify a particularly relaxing or enjoyable experience.**
- **Recall what you saw,** what colors were present, whether it was bright or dark, what objects were in your field of vision, whether there was motion or stillness in what you saw.
- **Recall what you heard,** what kind of tone the sounds had, whether it was loud or quiet, rhythmic or not.
- **Recall what you felt** at the time, the temperature of the air, what position your body was in, what your skin felt like, what kind of emotional or internal feelings you may have had.
- **Recall what you tasted or smelled** at the time, whether it was sweet or sour or bitter, strong or mild.
- **Run through each sense and increase the intensity in your mind**—make the colors brighter, the sounds clearer or louder, and the feelings stronger.
- **Enjoy your experience** and explore it in whatever way is comfortable.

✧✧✧

In this exercise, the details of memory serve as anchors that help to elicit the state. You may also be able to notice which sensory details take you further and more pleasurably into the relaxing or enjoyable experience.

Transderivational Search

While exploring these exercises, you may have noticed a tendency for your mind to sort through a range of memories and associations before selecting a single one to work with. This state-related phenomenon is called *transderivational search.*[8] For instance, in the previous exercise, when asked to "identify a particularly relaxing or enjoyable experience," several (or many) related experiences may come to mind, their commonality being some aspects of state—that these experiences were, to some degree or another, "relaxing or enjoyable." Many of the exercises in this book begin by eliciting transderivational search and the instructions use deliberately vague language to help bring some part of this search into your conscious awareness. So when you encounter a suggestion such as "choose a particularly pleasant and powerful experience" or to remember a time when "you felt relaxed, resourceful, and you enjoyed yourself," you may find yourself playing with the process for a moment or two, attempting to fit some of your own memories into those parameters. That's okay. The techniques will typically work with any experience or memory that has a kinesthetic component, some element of feeling, and whatever memory you eventually choose will produce some result. Come as close to the suggested parameters as you can. Remember that the *how,* "powerful and pleasant," may be more important here than the *what,* "eating chocolate ice cream at age five." The details of your reference experiences are used as natural anchors to the states. With practice, you can gain skill with the essentially magical process of selecting states via transderivational search.

In conversation with others, transderivational search is part of how we make sense out of what other people say. If someone says something vague like, "I fell in love. Do you know what that's like?" there is no way that we can ever know that our experience of love is anything like that of another person—but our mind sorts through our memories and we make our own delineations and definitions. Transderivational search can be initiated as we seek meaning for a variety of linguistic patterns, individual words, symbols, images, sounds, and feelings.

This process of internal search happens quite naturally throughout the day for most, if not all, humans. It can happen noticeably and obviously, or our minds can whiz through a wild range of associated memories in the blink of an eye, too fast for the conscious mind to glimpse. Transderivational search appears to be not only a natural shift in state by itself, but may also be a major component of how we change state in general.

When we re-access a particular state or feeling using natural or intentional anchors, the state dependent nature of our memory can make it very easy to recall and sort through similar experiences. For instance, if we find and elicit a feeling of joy, our minds become adept at finding other joyous memories. This suggests a method for finding and accessing resources:

Exercise 1.5 Transderivational Memories

- **Recall an experience of a powerful and pleasant state** (or whatever resource state you choose to work with) using the "Hypnotic Memories" method.
- **Pay attention to the feeling** associated with the state. Enjoy it.
- **While enjoying the pleasant feeling, let your mind find other memories in which you had a similar feeling.** Notice how these additional memories are accessed—whether they come easily, which senses are involved, what information you can recall that you haven't thought of in a while, and so on.
- **Explore these phenomena with other states and feelings.** Notice if there are any similarities in the way your mind accesses additional memories. That is, while the content of the memories may be similar or different—how does your mind present the memories to you?

two

Form and Content

How or What?

Woohoo is more of a *how* than a *what*. The form that our perception and memory takes determines our emotional response at least as much as, if not more than, the content. For instance, state dependency suggests that when we are in a dark mood, it becomes difficult to see the bright side of things. And when we are in a sunny mood, we interpret our perceptions in that light.

The visual metaphors above were deliberately chosen. Perceptual subtleties called *submodalities* are used by our minds to tag and categorize our memories and stored experiences. Sensory submodalities are the finer distinctions that we make within a sense. For instance, in the visual sense, submodalities might include brightness, color, contrast, location of the recalled image, size of the image, and so forth. Auditory submodalities would include volume, tone, pitch, and tempo, among others. Kinesthetic submodalities might include distinctions such as temperature, pressure, movement, or whether or not the feeling was tactile or visceral.

If you were to recall a favorite memory now, you can notice any number of ways that the memory is different from the original experience. The representations that you make in your mind may be smaller, larger, louder, softer, nearer, farther, warmer, or cooler than the original experience. There may be more emphasis on the foreground of the mental image, or the background. It may be more transparent or more opaque, fuzzier or sharper. These are not only your mind's way of making sure that you can distinguish between memory and external reality, the subtleties of submodalities can also tag memories with information. If you highlight a passage in a book, the different hue marks out the phrase as more important; more subtly, if your clothes are neatly pressed, it may denote professionalism.

Similarly, we tend to express our likes and dislikes, among much else, through the way we encode submodalities onto memories. The way we do this is unique for everyone. In general, though, we might make our representations of memories and things that we like bigger, closer, brighter, louder, warmer, etc., and the representations of memories and things that we don't like smaller, farther, dimmer, softer, colder, etc. These sensory subtleties are frequently expressed in language as metaphor. Something important to us is *big*, something of great consequence might be *heavy*, someone intelligent might be considered *brilliant*, someone emotionally unavailable might be perceived as *distant*, or you may feel *close* to someone you like.[1] Again, which qualities represent what ideas is different for everyone; these are just examples.

Here's a simple exercise to help understand this process:

Exercise 2.1 Comparing Submodalities

- **Think of two things that are qualitatively very similar,** but you nonetheless prefer one and dislike another. For instance, you might like Coke but not Pepsi, or you might like pullover sweaters but not ones with buttons, oak trees but not maple trees, etc.
- **Addressing first the thing you dislike and then the thing you like, take a few minutes and notice how you represent it.** Do you make an internal image? Do you place that image close to you or far away? Is it bright or dim? Are there sounds in your memory of this thing? Are they close or far? Loud or soft? Rhythmic or tonal? Words or sounds? Are there feelings in your internal representation? Do they involve temperature, pressure, movement, and so on? Where are the feelings located?
- **Notice the differences between the submodalities that you used to represent the thing or memory that you liked and the one that you didn't like.**

If you are like most people, there was some difference. It might be in any one of the submodality categories. It may be subtle or it may be quite obvious. However you represented these memories or things, your mind recognizes and utilizes submodality distinctions on an unconscious level. The submodalities are like little tags that your mind uses to remind you that these memories are close to you, important to you, a big issue, and so on.

So the question now becomes, "What sensory-based metaphors, what submodalities, express woohoo for you?" Do you feel your most woohoo when your experience is radiant, dark, vast, infinitesimal, harmonious, to the beat of a different drummer, close, far, all around, nowhere to be seen, tingly, soft, unfathomably deep, everywhere to be seen, cool, hot, sweet, pungent, expansive, silent, or spectacular? (Or something else, of course.)

Comparing internal representations that we make in different states can offer some important clues to the nature of woohoo. Make yourself comfortable and take a few minutes to learn about your own use of submodalities in the following way:

Exercise 2.2 Finding the Sweet Spots

- **Find a neutral experience for calibration purposes,** a memory or recalled object, place or person that you have little or no interest in, either positively or negatively. Notice how you represent this memory. Is it primarily visual, auditory, kinesthetic, gustatory, olfactory, or some combination of senses? Where do you place the memory? (Remember, we are discussing the form of our thoughts here, not the content of the memory. So the answer to the question is probably not "In the hot tub;" it is more likely to be something like "Off to my left and down a little," or "right in front of me.") Is it large, small, close, far, loud, soft, bright, or dim?

- **Think about something that absolutely turns you on,** floats your boat, lights your fire, blows you away, impresses the hell out of you, or that you otherwise really, really like. Again, map out the way that you represent this thought to yourself. Is it primarily visual, auditory, kinesthetic, gustatory or olfactory, or some combination of senses? Where do you place the memory? Is it large, small, close, far, loud, soft, bright, or dim?
- **Think about something of which you are absolutely certain.** Choose a thought that is very fundamental to your beliefs about the world. The sun will rise in the morning. Air is good to breathe. We are on Planet Earth. Food is necessary for life. Make the thought as fundamental and *certain* as possible. Notice how you represent this thought. Is it primarily visual, auditory, kinesthetic, gustatory or olfactory, or some combination of senses? Where do you place the memory? Is it large, small, close, far, loud, soft, bright, or dim?
- **Remember the person that you love most in the whole world.** Map out the submodalities of that representation.

- **Remember a peak experience that changed your life** and notice the submodalities involved in how you present this to yourself.
- **Write down** or otherwise record this information so that you can notice the differences between the neutral calibration experience and each of the more woohooful thoughts.
- **Experiment with using this information to add woohoo to less exciting thoughts.** Is there an experience you'd like to learn to enjoy more thoroughly? Practice thinking about it in the way that you did the experience that "turns you on" and "floats your boat." Move the representation of what you'd like to enjoy into the location, size, brightness, volume, etc., of your turned-on memory. Is there something you'd like to be more certain of in your life? Think about it in terms of the submodalities you found for your "certain" experience. Someone you want to feel more love for? Practice thinking about them with "love" submodalities. An experience you want to have more impact in your life? Give your thoughts about it the submodalities of a "peak experience." If it helps, think about these experiments as "trying on" the altered experiences and remember that you can always change them back to how they were.

Please note that the point of this exercise is not necessarily to change your life in a sweeping gesture (we'll get to that soon!), but simply to notice how the way you represent your thoughts, memories and experiences influences the way you feel about them. For now, consider this: do you think your chances for success, fun, satisfaction, or whatever your goals are, might be improved with more excitement, certainty, love, or life-changing power?

What Your Brain Does When You Aren't Looking

The human brain's tendency to tag memories with submodalities is an ongoing process that involves transderivational search. Indeed, it may well be that every time your mind searches through a stack of interrelated memories, on an unconscious level you may be organizing, cataloging, and tagging the memories at the same time. The first bit of neurological lore that falls into place here is the concept of *memory reconsolidation*. This is the idea that every time we call up a memory and then send it back into storage, it may change a little bit.[2] Another bit of relevant brain theory concerns what our neurology starts doing when we aren't consciously directing it.

In 2001, a team of researchers at Washington University School of Medicine in St. Louis, led by Marcus Raichle, identified what they believed to be a new system in the brain.[3] The group was attempting to define a baseline state for brain activity. That is, they wanted to know what the brain was doing when its owner wasn't doing anything. Once determined, a baseline could be used as comparison with other neurological functions that were being studied. They arranged for subjects to be observed with PET scans and, later, fMRI tools when they were actively doing something with their mind and when they were just, you know, spacing out. (By measuring changes in blood flow, fMRI technology can monitor brain activity in real time.)

But they found something a little weirder than they were expecting. When the brain is not consciously aimed toward a specific activity, you might think that it would go into a kind of rest mode. If it were a computer, the hard drive might power down and the screen saver would come on. However, Raichle and his team found that, rather than powering down, a collection of structures along the midline of the brain—"cortical midline structures"—actually power up. It was odd because when the experimental subjects weren't consciously doing anything, their brains began to use more power and actually consumed nearly 30 percent more calories than "active" brains.

They dubbed this collection of structures in the brain the *default network* and they, and many other neurological researchers, set about trying to figure out just what, exactly, all these parts of the brain were doing with each other. Now all these brain areas had been studied before, but it was becoming apparent that when conscious activity and external awareness were limited, these structures linked up and started chattering among themselves.

One of the major components involved in the default network is the medial prefrontal cortex, where our minds apply value judgments to things from a self-centered point of view. This is the part of the brain that decides if something is good, bad, or indifferent; if we like something or not; if an experience has woohoo or not. Another major component of the default network is the hippocampus, a part of the brain where, among other things, we temporarily store and sort through personal memories.

The default network is activated when simply spacing out, daydreaming, and *when stimuli prompt the brain to search through stored memories.* Are you catching on to the process we're describing here? That's right, just out of sight of your conscious awareness, it seems that the default network flips the switch on transderivational search, tags memories using submodalities, and then reconsolidates the altered memories into what is essentially the story of your life. In effect, submodalities become the language by which the parts of the default network communicate among themselves and with other parts of the brain.

Mystical Brain Language

Now if we, as magicians, want to consciously direct changes to the way that we perceive our selves and our world, we might find it useful to learn and use the "brain language" of submodalities. Luckily, we already know it—it's a part of us. The trick to using it, however, is more a matter of separating it out from the sensory details of content.

The use of submodality information removed from its usual context has formed a part of occult and mystical teaching for millennia. Concepts such as chi, prana, and kundalini are usually imagined and manipulated as colored (or colorless) light. Vibration, harmony, tingling, rushing, glowing, auras, halos, stillness, smallness, vastness, all terms commonly used to describe mystical or peak experience, are essentially submodality descriptions. The sensory language of mystical literature reaches its purest form with descriptions of boundless light, white light, astral bells, and open-ended descriptions of pure sounds, visions, feelings, and so on. Aleister Crowley described one of his pivotal mystical experiences as "Nothingness with twinkles," for instance.[4] Memories marked by glowing, soft expansiveness, for example, may be identified (by some) as sacred. Thoughts tagged with rushing, huge, sparkles, perhaps, might denote woohoo. **Changes in sensory submodalties denote change in state.**[5]

At the more practical end of occult practice and "psychic energy work," imagining colored geometric shapes and symbols in and around the body conveys information on an unconscious level through submodality (size, shape, color, brightness, location, movement, etc.) while the symbols themselves may convey information by association and transderivational search. Similarly, the practices of visualizing chakras, sephira, and channels of energy through the spinal column and body rely on metaphoric sensory "brain language" to effect specific changes in state.

While this model of "energy work" addresses the mystical energies of the human life force as metaphors that describe neurological processes, these must still be experienced or imagined as energy, light, temperature, color, shape, movement, fluid, or whatever to alter state and produce results. (And ultimately, we are describing the action of consciousness, whether we decide chi is an actual energy or the attention of the human mind.) A possible limitation of the traditional methods is that they often have a one-size-fits-all approach. In some systems, for instance, chakras are rainbow-colored and magical pentagrams are blue, for one and all. Orbits of energy in the body always flow in one direction to benefit health and mood. A black aura means depression; a white one means spirituality, and so forth. The difficulty here is when these colors, sizes, directions, and other distinctions are offered without any attempt to calibrate for the individual. The psyches of humans vary as much as our fingerprints or tax returns; there's no guarantee that a black aura will mean the same thing for everyone or that blue pentagrams will induce the same state for different magicians. Just a few minutes of practice and observation can reveal our own personal "brain language" and easily increase the applicability and effectiveness of chi, prana, and every last drop of kundalini. Balance your chakras with woohoo!

We've already played with one method for identifying natural energy flows. The following exercise expands on the practice of Energy Flow Modeling and can be a fantastic way to change and manage state any time we choose.

Exercise 2.3 Energy Flow Modeling

Choose a particularly pleasant and powerful experience that you've had. Recall the experience in as much detail as possible in the following manner:

- **Remember what you saw** when you were having the experience. Notice any motion or stillness in your field of vision. Notice the quality of the light and the quality of the colors. Notice if the things you see are near or far away.
- **Remember what you heard** when you were having the experience. Notice any sounds or silence. Notice if the sounds are loud or quiet, and if they are tones, rhythms, or voices. Notice any background sounds in the environment of your memory.
- **Remember what you felt** at the time. Remember what position your body was in, and if you were moving or still. Remember the temperature of the air on your skin.

- As you continue to recall more details of the experience, **notice where in your body the pleasant feeling begins** and where it moves to as the experience develops. **Notice what kind of a feeling it is**—if it is temperature, tingling, pressure, movement, texture, or however you might experience it.
- **Give the feeling a color or colors.** If this feeling had a color, what would it be? Apply that color or colors everywhere in your body that you identify the feeling.
- **Notice the shape and movement of the color** in your body. For a state to maintain over time, it needs to cycle or pulse. If yours is cycling or pulsing, then accentuate that cycle or pulse, make it move faster or bigger, or whatever enhances your experience. If your experience is not already cycling or pulsing, then imagine that it is … loop it back around so that it forms a cycle, then accentuate that cycle. This is called an **Energy Flow.**
- **Accentuate it even more.** Fill your entire body with the color, from head to toe. Make the colors richer, more vibrant. Add sparkles, shimmers, or glows if they increase the intensity of the experience.
- **Enjoy** for as long as you'd like.

Of course, now that you know how to create a sensory metaphor for your experiences, you can change and influence them as well. The following is yet another exercise demonstrating how changes in submodality are associated with changes in state and also how very useful this knowledge can be.

Exercise 2.4 Energy Flow/Reversal of Flow

- **Select a mildly unpleasant experience** that you have had. (This can be used with more unpleasant and even truly awful experiences, but for the purposes of learning, select a mildly unpleasant experience.)
- **Create an energy flow** from the unpleasant experience as you did with the pleasant experience in Energy Flow Modeling. Notice how it cycles or cause it to cycle, but do not accentuate.
- **Reverse the direction of the cycle** or pulse. Note how your experience of the feeling has changed, then accentuate by increasing the speed or size of the cycle.
- **Accentuate it even more.** Fill your entire body with the color, from head to toes. Make the colors richer, more vibrant. Add sparkles, shimmers, or glows if they increase the intensity of the experience.
- **Enjoy** for as long as you'd like.

Remember that the purpose at this point is not necessarily to perform miraculous feats of change—though that's fun, too—but to learn a little bit about the way your brain encodes information via sensory metaphor. Repeating the exercises with a variety of pleasant and unpleasant memories may offer clues as to what colors and movements are associated with certain feelings for you. Likewise, accentuating and modifying the energy flows can really begin to take you toward your personal woohoo. Unlike the dogmatically offered colors, symbols, shapes, and directions of historical methods, what you can learn through these experiments will be based directly in your own tendencies and neurology. These are *your* chakras, *your* energy meridians, *your* own aura with its own colors and symbolism. If you do prefer to work with traditional methods, the information gained from a bit of applied woohoology can be used to subtly—or dramatically—tune up your practice.

Creating Anchors

Energy flows can be their own anchors. That is, recalling the shape, size, movement, direction, color, and brightness of the flow can lead you back into the state. It is also quite easy to intentionally create and use additional anchors while working with energy flows. The following exercises represent one way of creating and working with a physical anchor.

Exercise 2.5 Energy Flow/Gesture

- **Select an experience you've had in which you felt really, really good.**
- **Develop an energy flow** from it as in the previous exercises.
- When you have accentuated the flow and intensified the feeling, **express the feeling as a simple gesture or movement.**
- **Practice making the gesture** and enjoy the good feeling.

- **Wait until later**, when you are outside the context of this experiment, **and make the gesture** or movement. **Note what happens.**

Anchors can be associated with our experiences and our lives in numerous ways. The following is a simple method to use an anchor/gesture to carry specific states into your future.

Exercise 2.6 Future-paced Gesture

- **Select a powerful and positive feeling of resourcefulness**, a memory of an experience that you have had in which you felt relaxed, resourceful, and you enjoyed yourself.
- **Create an energy flow and a gesture** for this resourceful feeling, as in the previous exercise.
- **Practice making the gesture** and enjoy the good feeling.
- Pause for moment and then **select some upcoming situation in your life about which you may experience anxiety**, trepidation, or otherwise feel uncomfortable.
- **Make your gesture again.** As you are making the gesture and enjoying the feeling, **try to think about the upcoming situation.** Note what happens.
- Cease making the gesture and then **try to think about the upcoming situation.** Note what happens.
- **Repeat as necessary** throughout your life.

Again, the anchors that you create with the methods outlined here will be based in the tendencies of your own organism and will be uniquely applicable to the states you explore. The subtleties of the gesture's movements provide their own sensory-rich metaphor to describe state, much as traditional magical gestures symbolize concepts and states. How much woohoo can you express with a gesture?

Woohoo can often be experienced in the company of others and energy flows can be shared and merged in a variety of ways. In fact, we usually do develop energy flows with other people naturally in most social situations. The following exercise is a great way to learn how to move this usually unconscious process into awareness, so that it comes under your conscious control.

Exercise 2.7 Partner Flow

- **Partners face each other and take several deep breaths** together.
- **Each individual thinks about a particularly pleasant and empowering experience** they may have had recently or in the past.
- **Each develops an energy flow** as in previous exercises and accentuates it in whatever way proves to be most enjoyable.
- **Partners explain their flows to each other,** describing size, color, movement, direction, and location, without making mention of the original reference memories.

- **Partners collaborate on a way to join the energy flows.** This is accomplished by letting one flow into the other so that it becomes one single energy flow moving through both people. Let each individual determine what it looks and feels like when it is inside them; just link the cycle of the flow.
- Partners **enjoy** the cycle for a few minutes.
- **Partners separate the flow** into two separate flows again, then each individual takes a deep breath and **ends the practice.**

Notice that in this exercise, individuals are encouraged to interpret the qualities of the energy flow for themselves, while it cycles through them. Remember that we each may use different metaphors to describe similar experiences. With a little bit of imagination, this exercise can be adapted in numerous ways to fit the people and circumstances involved. For instance, think about the physical location of the partners. Participants can be back-to-back, side-to-side, or facing each other, and can be at a distance or in physical contact. Indeed, mutual energy flows can be used to prolong and intensify erotic encounters in a variety of physical positions. Woohoo!

three

Invocation and Evocation

Inside Out

Principal among the operations of magick are *invocation* and *evocation*. Invocation is the act of drawing qualities or entities into you; evocation is the act of perceiving entities or qualities as external forms. Invocation rituals are often devotional. You go into the temple of the Goddess of Good Fortune and gaze upon her image and perform acts of worship in her honor so that something of good fortune may enter into your life. Some religions tell stories about their gods, sing songs, paint pictures, create stained-glass windows, and build cathedrals to imbue worshippers with godly feelings.

Evocation rituals are typified by the "summoning of spirits," calling entities forth, external to the magician, so that the magician can communicate with the entity or induce it to go out into the world and perform various tasks. Better known systems of evocation include the Goetia, based on the *Keys of Solomon,*[1] and the practices associated with *The Book of the Sacred Magick of Abramelin the Mage.*[2]

It's pretty simple to remember: *IN*vocation is the drawing *IN* of qualities or entities; Evocation is about relating to qualities or entities *E*xternal to oneself. That's where the simplicity ends, however. Hold on to your hat while your cognitive functions take a little ride though the ambiguity of consciousness. In general, most (if not all) of what we take for "the world" is a "user illusion," a way that our brain interprets the world that allows us to experience clouds of probability (as physicists explain the nature of subatomic particles) as solid matter. We perceive the surface of our skin (however permeable and, ultimately, created of those clouds of probability and space) as the boundary between self and world. And we make numerous similarly illusory representations of everything we've ever seen, heard, felt, tasted, or smelled. Consider our experience of the world as a map or model that we create with our thoughts (and some help from the brain's default network), based on the interpretation of our perception. *Whether or not there is an objective reality to bump up against, all we can ever really do is experience our mind's interpretation of bumping.*[3] And this model-making most certainly includes the delineation we make between ourselves and the rest of the world. What we consider to be internal and external may just be convenient distinctions that help us to maintain a sense of self and to navigate what we perceive of the world.

For practical purposes, we usually find that we need to take our internal representation *as* the world. So, for the time being, we can play within the usual rules and relate to our books or reading devices as solid objects, decide that we are something separate from the air we breathe, and treat as "unreal" only those things we recognize as figments of our imagination. Good with that? Are we still messing with ambiguity if we place imaginary objects or entities external to us or inside us? When invoking the Goddess of Good Fortune, we change our experience as if she has entered us, even though she probably only existed in our minds. When evoking the Goetic demon Barbas, we treat this highly imaginary entity as if it were a sentient creature external to us. It's our experience, we get to define how we relate to it—one of the perks of being alive—and it is pretty much the same game we play, on an unconscious level, with just about everything else in our world that we decide is in us or outside us, real or not real, fun or not fun, woohoo or not woohoo.

All right, then. We'll put the ambiguity of world-modeling and personal boundaries aside. For now, consider internal/external as a simple submodality distinction, one more way that our brain hangs a tag on perceptions to make them useful, to integrate them into our personal narrative, or to imbue experiences with woohoo.

Dr. Milton Erickson once said that hypnotic trance was the controlled use of "**the same mental mechanisms that are operative spontaneously in everyday life**."[4] The operations of magick are likewise operative in everyday life. Both invocation and evocation appear to be natural functions of human consciousness. If you have ever gazed at artwork, read a book, or listened to music in order to experience a particular emotion, mood, or feeling, you have performed an act of invocation. Did you have an imaginary friend when you were a child? Or do you ever imagine other people when you daydream? These are acts of evocation. Attributing sentience to otherwise inanimate objects can also be described as a form of evocation. What? You've never cursed at your computer or verbally encouraged your car?

Relating to our perceptual representations, whether internal or external, as sentient beings takes these naturally occurring behaviors and brings them up to their full, magical form. Even this happens spontaneously. Have you ever dreamed about someone you know? They may or may not behave exactly like the waking version of the person, but, nonetheless, dream characters seem sentient, self-motivated, and even unpredictable. This ability to create minds within our own consciousness appears to be based in neurology.

Monkeys and Mirror Neurons

A chance discovery in the late 1980s may have revealed part of how our minds conceive of entities. Three researchers at the University of Parma in Italy, Giacomo Rizzolatti, Leonardo Fogassi, and Vittorio Gallese, were studying hand movements in macaque monkeys. They had a monkey wired up with electrodes to measure brain activity in the inferior frontal cortex, paying close attention to an area of motor neurons that became active when the monkey was grabbing, pushing, picking things up, and so forth. When researcher Fogassi reached toward a bowl of fruit and picked up a banana, that area of monkey brain cells lit up, just as if the little fellow had reached for the fruit himself—but the monkey hadn't actually moved a muscle!

That is, just by observing someone reaching for a banana, the monkey was experiencing, for himself, what that would be like.[5]

The experiment was repeated by the original researchers and by others with similar results. More recently, experiments in humans confirmed that we, too, have a "mirror neuron system" that is activated in our brains when we observe other people.[6] This means that, to some extent, it is possible to feel someone else's pain (or joy or dyspepsia or satisfaction), walk a mile in their moccasins, or, literally, share a laugh. It also explains why we enjoy watching actors in movies and athletes in games—as we watch, our own brains are experiencing almost as if we were the character on the screen or the player on the field and we get to share in the emotion or exhilaration. Mirror neurons offer a clue to the phenomena of the contact high, why the designated driver giggles like an idiot along with everyone else, and why yawns are contagious. And perhaps we've also solved the mystery of why air guitar is so much fun.

The human brain, not surprisingly, is a lot more complex than that of the macaque. We won't write off monkey complexity just yet, though. An experimental follow-up to the original fruit-grabbing routine placed a piece of cardboard between the monkey and the fruit bowl, blocking the view. When a researcher reached toward the fruit bowl, behind the cardboard, the monkey's mirror neurons were still activated. The macaque had imagined the fruit theft and responded as if it had actually seen the crime in progress—which meant that it also felt as if it were swiping the banana itself. *Imagination can activate mirror neurons*, even in monkey brains.[7]

In humans, mirror neurons share space with areas of the brain responsible for language, as well as simple movements.[8] Speech, sign language, and written language will all stimulate mirror neurons. It helps us to empathize with the speaker or writer. A great orator's words can stir us to action; a novel's narrator can feel like an old friend. Just as the monkey can imagine a hand grabbing a banana, we more complex humans can imagine fictional characters, imaginary friends, gods, demons, and memetic entities—and we can be moved by them.

We'll refer to this process as *Entity Modeling*, the ability to recognize and represent qualities and states as entities. In 1950, early computer scientist Alan Turing speculated that machines could be said to achieve artificial intelligence if and when its communication could not be distinguished from a human. Turing proposed a test in which an interrogator sat before two terminals, a human communicating through one by typing and a computer through the other. If the interrogator could not tell the difference, the machine would then be considered an artificial intelligence. An intuitive Turing Test, if you will, performed by the mirror neurons, seems to immediately categorize things into "conscious entity" and "inanimate lump." We look at each other and, hopefully, we recognize another human as both conscious and at least reasonably intelligent. Some very simple visual patterns, for instance, seem to fire off this sense of recognition—a smiley face, have-a-nice day symbol is recognizable to us as a human face; a *South Park* cartoon character can be identified with, at least for a half hour at a time, as a conscious entity with the ability to communicate, make decisions, and act, however stupidly, upon the world. Linguistic patterns also seem to have a similar ability. A sentence formed with proper syntax suggests that its writer or speaker possesses some measure of intelligence. Whereas a formed with sentence syntax that proper its suggests little or nothing. Based on such unconscious intuitions, we recognize writers as conscious entities when we read their well-formed sentences. We recognize other humans as such when we communicate with each other in text environments such as Internet forums. And we even recognize fictional characters as entities for whom we might predict behavior and sympathize. There are likely also many other behavioral patterns and cues that help us to, unconsciously, tell the difference between a conscious entity and a brick of cheese.

Symbols that represent entities affect our neurology similarly to the entities themselves. Just as the shape of a cartoon might tell us, in an obvious way, that the representation is intended to be an entity, the shape of an energy flow will tell us, perhaps on a more unconscious level, information about the entity it represents.

Evocation

Are we the same people all the time? Each state we pass through has its own kind of intelligence, its own kind of logic, its own reality tunnel. The quick snapshot of consciousness that we call a state can be thought of as an internal model of an entity, the person who you were then. The energy flow is a metaphoric representation of that entity. When we evoke an energy flow, externalizing it so that we can communicate with it, we refer to it as a *state entity*. State entities are rich sources of information about our lives and ready power sources for ritual and personal change.

Magical rituals of evocation range from the deep, mysterious and complex to the extremely simple. The following evocation techniques are about as simple as it gets, and offer you a chance to meet your state entities.

Exercise 3.1 Simple Evocations[9]

Basic Positive Resource Entity

- **Banishing**—Imagine a circle around you, where you sit. Take a deep breath. As you inhale, let your awareness fill the circle. As you exhale, let your awareness contract to as small a point as you can, in the center of your chest. After five or six cycles of this, take a really, really, really deep breath, filling the circle with your awareness, then exhale forcefully and fully, letting (or imagining) your breath sweep through your personal circle, chasing out anything contrary to your purpose.
- **Evocation**—Identify something in your life that makes you feel very good in some way. It can be a feeling of confidence, intelligence, satisfaction, arousal, intoxication, approval, or whatever you might describe as a good feeling. Pay very careful attention to HOW it makes you feel, the structure of the feeling. Where does the feeling start? What kind of feeling is it? Where does it go as it develops? Does it continue to move? Is it static? Follow it through to its peak. Then decide "If this feeling had a color, what would it be?" Imagine the color (or colors) in your body in exactly the areas where the feeling is experienced. Then imagine that you are taking

the colored shape out of your body and flip it around to face you. Place it on the floor outside your circle and breathe deeply, feeding it breath and energy on each exhalation.

- **Keep breathing and feeding it energy** until it transforms. It may change shape, size, color, movement, or may take an entirely different form. Once it has transformed, imagine you are communicating with it. Ask it what it wants to be called. Ask it what it can teach you that it has never before revealed. Ask it how you can feel really good more often. Find out whatever you can from it. Thank it for everything.
- You can also ask this entity if it has anything that it would like to do, away from your physical body, off in the external parts of consciousness. If it says that it does, then you can get an agreement of time from the entity—five minutes, an hour, a day, five years, or whatever is appropriate to the task—and the promise from the entity to return to your physical presence at that time. Note down the time of the entity's return so that you can take notice when it occurs. Ask that your entity will choose to do this only if it is in your benefit and that it will be working on your behalf no matter where it is.
- **Closing**—Absorb the entity, if it has remained with you, and anything else you may have created in your aura during this operation.
- Repeat **Banishing**.

Transforming Negative Entities

- **Banishing**—Imagine a circle around you, where you sit. Take a deep breath. As you inhale, let your awareness fill the circle. As you exhale, let your awareness contract to as small a point as you can, in the center of your chest. After five or six cycles of this, take a really, really, really deep breath, filling the circle with your awareness, and then exhale forcefully and fully, letting (or imagining) your breath sweep through your personal circle, chasing out anything contrary to your purpose.
- **Evocation**—Identify something in your life that makes you feel bad in some way. This technique can be used even with major trauma. It is recommended, however, that you begin with less intense experiences until you develop proficiency. For your first time, think about something in your life that is mildly unpleasant. A situation with family members or coworkers that leaves you feeling annoyed, for instance.
- Again, notice where the feeling flows in your body and **mark it out with colors** as you did for the good feeling in the "Basic Positive Resource Entity" exercise. **Flip it around and place it outside the circle**, in front of you, but this time trap it in a geometric shape of some kind, a triangle or square drawn (in your imagination) on the floor.
- **Keep breathing and feeding it energy** until it transforms. Again, it may change shape, size, color, movement, or may take an entirely different

form. Once it has transformed, imagine you are communicating with it. Ask it what it wants to be called. Ask it what it wants. Ask if there's a way to accomplish that goal in a more pleasant manner. Negotiate. Find out what it can do for you that it hasn't done before. Find out what you can do for it. Keep breathing to feed it energy. It may transform again if your negotiation is successful—in which case, flip it back around and draw it back into your body, in its original position. If it doesn't change again, you have a couple of choices: 1) draw it back into yourself, but reversed from its original position; or 2) breathe and draw some energy from it with your inhalation until it has diminished somewhat, then reabsorb it back, flipped around to its original position.

- Repeat **Banishing**.

So far, we've been communicating with our state entities pretty much as we find them. Remember that these are our own self-metaphors and that they can change and adapt as our imagination directs. It is possible to create entities that are targeted for very specific purposes. We will explore a number of ways to customize entities in the coming pages. Here is one way to create entities with simple evocation that may help us understand or resolve many different issues in our lives.

Exercise 3.2 Customizing an Entity

- **Banish.**
- **Evoke a state entity** either from a positive resource state or from a "bad feeling," as above.
- When the entity is outside your body, **ask it what it would like to be called and what it wants.**
- **Find the "purpose behind the purpose."** Take its response about what it wants and ask, "What do you get from that that is more important?" For instance, if the entity says it wants you to relax, you can ask, "What do you get from relaxation that is more important than relaxation?" And **keep asking until the answers seem to reach a "highest level" of personal criteria.** These often deal with overall mission, spirituality, or sense of identity. For instance, in response to "What do you get from relaxation?" the answer is "Good health," you would ask "What do you get from good health that is more important than good health?" The answer might be "Ability to do your job." "What do you get from the ability to do your job that is more important than the ability to do your job?" And so on, until you have reached the highest level of criteria that you can.[10]
- Keep the state entity externalized where it is, and using the highest level response you got from it, **create a second energy flow in yourself that represents that particular criteria,** the best you can. Use a personal memory of

that kind of experience or, if you can't find a personal memory of your own, think about what it would feel like to be someone else who has that kind of experience. Identify the feeling, give it a color, etc.

- **Externalize the second energy flow and add it to the state entity** that was previously evoked. Notice any changes that may happen.
- **Communicate with the entity** and confirm that any changes that have happened will fit happily (or usefully) with your experience and your life.
- **Bring the combined/transformed entity back into your body** as in the previous exercises.
- **Banish.**

Sometimes you need multiple resources as you walk your path in life. Here is one way to literally line up a collection of resources and start to apply them to your future. Like the previous exercises, you can do this next one entirely in your imagination, but it can become much more powerful if you actually get up and move physically through the ritual.

Exercise 3.3 Walking Through States

- **Banish.**
- Using the above methods, **create a series of different state entities that represent at least three resourceful states** (states in which you feel good, powerful, creative,

intelligent, strong, compassionate, patient, or similarly resourceful).

- **Place the entities** in positions where they are separate from each other, but **where you can easily walk through them** with just a step or two in between each.
- **Select a situation in your life** in which you could use some insight or new resources.
- **Think about that situation as you step successively into each state entity.** Notice what different aspects of the situation come to mind in each different position. Notice what different kinds of thoughts you have about the situation in each different position. Leave each entity in its place as you step toward and into the next one.
- Step out from all the entities and then **absorb them back into you.**
- **Banish.**

This exercise also demonstrates how we can anchor states to physical positions or locations. A fun variation on Walking Through States might be to leave some of these state entities in various places where you will have to walk through them during the course of the day. You might find it useful to walk through the Wide Awake state entity on your way into the kitchen in the morning, or into a Focused and Professional state entity as you enter your office for a day of work, for instance.

four

Mirror Realities

Theory of Mind

Remember the personal narrative, that full-sensory story, that your default network spins behind the scenes? While mirror neurons use motor areas of the brain to internally replicate actions, cortical midline structures have the ability to model or represent your whole mind, your whole body, indeed, your whole life. Through a medium of memory, states, and submodality markers, your brain composes the story of your life, complete with character development, backstory, and an entire world in which it can play. That same engine of modeling, with the power to represent a complete mind, also comes into action when we make our internal representations of others. The mirror neurons help us begin the process by recognizing other people as being like us and understanding their movements and intentions. From there, the default network can develop complex psychological models. This ability is called *Theory of Mind* and allows us to not only empathize but to make detailed projections of another person's thought and behavior. Mirror neurons conspire with the cortical midline structures of the default network to bring us the rich and detailed world of imagination.[1] And, as already noted, our imaginings can activate our neurology and physiology as if they were "real."

There's a natural purpose for this mental activity. In effect, evidence suggests that when humans get social, we are interacting as much with these internal models of each other as with the actual people they represent. It is part of how we relate to each other all the time. There are quite a few predictions that we make about each others' behavior, for instance, that are complex, yet so fundamental to our behavior that we take them for granted. The simple, motor-neuron behaviors may be the most obvious. For example, if someone offers you a glass of water, you automatically and unconsciously make detailed predictions about how they will follow through, where they will go, where the glass will end up, and anything else that helps enable you to meet and receive the glass with your own hand. Beyond the simple monkey tricks, though, we also make more elaborate social predictions about whether someone will respond appropriately to a joke, if it is the right time to shake hands (which involves social prediction as well as motor prediction), and what kind of efforts will most please employers, friends, and family members. Whether these predictions are entirely accurate or not, they are parts of the model on which we base our decisions and actions.

Indeed, the nature of the model sometimes becomes painfully apparent when our communication goes awry. For instance, consider the mighty provider for his family who buys his wife houses, cars, and boats, but she leaves him anyway because all she wanted was to spend some time with him. These purely hypothetical people remain at odds because they each continue to operate on fallible maps of each others' mind. He thinks that property ownership will make her happy. She thinks he likes her company.

Sometimes we use the limits of human model-making to our advantage, as when a fighter feints in one direction and strikes from another, or when a stage magician uses misdirection to create an illusion. If a hapless opponent makes a faulty prediction about what the fighter intends, he gets clobbered. If an audience member acts on an inaccurate model of the magician's movements, she gets to be delighted by the illusion.

One of the fun things about imagination is that it is like breathing. Normally, most of the functions of imagination—social predictions, dreams, fantasy, and model-making in general—are largely unconscious processes. Like drawing your next breath, the processes continue without much conscious input at all. However, if you choose to take conscious control over your breathing or your imagination, you can direct it in any number of ways.

The most likely basis for the various models and projections we make about others begins with the models we make of ourselves—the personal narrative that constantly forms and reforms in our brains. Simple adjustments to that model can yield interesting, exciting, and even woohoo-filled experiences.

Associated/Dissociated

In every one of our senses, an important submodality distinction we can make is whether our experience can be considered "associated" or "dissociated." This is, perhaps, another way to approach internal/external distinctions: **Associated means that we experience the perception from our own frame of reference,** from our own point of view. **Dissociated means that we experience the perception as if from another frame of reference** or point of view. For example, in visual representations, an associated image would represent the experience as if from our own eyes. A dissociated visual representation would be as if we were someone else looking at ourselves. In the associated image, we would see what we saw, and in the dissociated image, we would see ourselves in the image as if looking in a mirror or watching ourselves on video.

Any sense can be represented as associated or dissociated. For example, you can say something, or you can imagine hearing your own voice. You can feel your present state inside your own body, or you can imagine feeling yourself as an external presence.

The following exercises involve using your imagination to adjust your own self-image. Remember, everyone visualizes, recalls sounds, or elicits feelings in their own unique ways. Do each to the best of your ability and remember that some imaginings may be naturally vague and some may be very rich in detail.

Exercise 4.1 In and Out

- **Notice what you see, hear, and feel now, from your own point of view. Then imagine what you might look like, sound like, or feel like to another person.**
- **Pay attention to any changes in your state** as you do this.
- **Recall a few significant experiences** in your life, both pleasant and (mildly) unpleasant.
- For each experience, **remember what you saw, heard, and felt,** and then…
- **Imagine what you would have looked like, sounded like, felt like to another person** (whether or not there was another person present in the memory).
- **Pay attention to any changes in your state** as you do this.

Exercise 4.2 Watch Yourself Relax

- **Imagine that you can see yourself, or hear yourself, or feel yourself, as if observing another person.** Make it like looking at a movie or a picture of yourself. If you are better at hearing or feeling, then hear yourself talking or making sounds, or feel where your presence would be.
- **Imagine that this other self that you are observing is in a very comfortable and very, very relaxing place.** It's not necessary to see,

hear, or feel the place, just keep your attention on this other self.

- **Watch, listen, and/or feel as this other self becomes more and more relaxed,** more and more comfortable, and exhibits the effects of relaxation: softer muscles, different posture, different facial expression, and so forth.
- **Make changes to the structure of the image** (but not the content):

  a. Make the image larger or smaller.

  b. Make the colors brighter or more muted.

  c. Emphasize the foreground as opposed to the background, and vice versa.

  d. Make the sounds or speech louder or quieter (if the emphasis is on hearing rather than seeing).

  e. Speed up and slow down the action (works for all senses).

  f. Move the image closer or farther away (works for all senses).

  g. Give the image a soft glow or sparkles.

- **Notice any changes to your state** as you experiment with these changes.

Notice how subtle changes in the structure of your imagined self, the alterations we make in the form and quality of our internal image, have the ability to change our response to the entity. Different configurations affect our consciousness in different ways. Making the representation larger or smaller, brighter or dimmer, etc., will often continue the process of making us more or less relaxed. Hopefully you found a configuration that was woohoofully relaxing.

The Neurological Origin of Gods

A few major pieces of our model are now in place. We know that mirror neurons and the cortical midline system of the default network can recognize and model entities in response to human-shaped images as well as words, sounds, feelings, and movements. Combined with the submodalities in which they are encoded, these images convey information about state. For most people, viewing these entity images can also nudge our neurology and physiology toward the state. Both the pure submodality information of energy flows and the human-shaped symbols can come pretty close to some of the traditional symbols used to access specific states. Those symbols are, of course, the gods, goddesses, demons, angels, and entities of every pantheon from every culture.

Indeed, some of the gods and goddesses of the ancient world not only look like us, but began their careers as human beings. This is perhaps most apparent in African and African Diaspora traditions where it is said that the Loas and Orishas once walked the Earth as our ancestors. By engaging in exploits that attained the level of legend, their lives became enshrined as tales and they transformed into beings of myth, memetic entities transmitted through stories, images, and rituals from mind to mind and from culture to culture. This is, potentially, the continuing memetic spread of states across big swaths of time.

Other historically important entities had human-shaped symbols created for them. The gods of nature were linguistic and iconic representations of the forces and secrets of the world around us. They were qualities that were given the faces, hands, bodies, words, and emotional experiences of humans so that we could appreciate them, discuss them, and share their states with others. Sometimes they are blended with animal or other non-human properties—for instance, the body of a lion on the Sphinx—but nonetheless include enough human-like cues to be recognized as entities.

In our culture, we have images, figures, and human-shaped symbols that we use for communicating and sharing states, but we don't necessarily call them gods. We call our important tales movies, books, comics, history, and journalism. We call their inhabitants fictional characters, superheroes, historical figures, and celebrities, among other things. When we contemplate our contemporary stories and the entities that populate them, as well as mythic tales of heroes and deities, we activate our neurology in ways that allow us to feel the joy, passion, sorrow, power, ethics, and wisdom of the gods. When we watch Luke Skywalker destroy the Death Star, we feel elation, almost as if we fired the decisive shot ourselves. When we look at the statue of Abraham Lincoln at the Lincoln Memorial in Washington, D.C., we may feel inspired by the wisdom and compassion of the great president. When we read a book or watch a movie about how Frodo Baggins carried the Ring to Mordor, we feel some of the excitement, horror, loyalty, and persistence that the fictional Frodo feels. When we see or hear our favorite rock stars, we feel something of the freedom and exuberance they transmit through their performance. We often use submodality language to describe what distinguishes these characters: "He is a shining example." "She is larger than life." "They went out in a blaze of glory."

What makes the difference between just another character, just another person, and the mythic beings that find a place in our pantheons? You guessed it—woohoo.

There are many ways to use these natural tendencies of consciousness for magical purposes. We can create and work with dissociated images in a way analogous to the use of traditional gods and goddesses. Let's start with one of the most common goals in practical magick—creating prosperity in our lives. Remember that prosperity is not necessarily about finances; for some people it might mean a happy family, a bountiful harvest, a big stamp collection, or a fully stocked store. Most often, prosperity is about the things that we hope to do to improve our lives.

Exercise 4.3 The Prosperity Technique[2]

- **Identify some of the challenges you have meeting the basic needs of your life.** What worrying thoughts occupy your mind? What aspects of your life take up inordinate amounts of time that would otherwise be devoted to your own work? What stresses you out?
- **Determine the opposites of those challenges.** If you are concerned with poverty, then the opposite may be sufficiency. If you are concerned with a difficult relationship, then the opposite may be a rewarding or pleasant relationship. And so on. These will be unique for you. For this exercise, avoid excess. Stick with the simplest opposite. For now we are simply addressing basic needs.

- **Breathe and banish.** Imagine a circle around yourself, at about the diameter of your spread arms. Sit or stand in the center of that circle. Fill your lungs completely, with a slow, even inhalation. As you inhale, allow your attention to expand to fill the circle. As you exhale slowly, evenly, and completely, allow your attention to contract to a single point in the center of your chest. Repeat at least three times.
- **Form a visual image of yourself, standing or sitting outside the circle.** Some people visualize more easily than others. If you find it easier to hear the sounds or voice of your imagined self or to feel your presence outside the circle, then begin with those senses. Then begin to fill in the other sensory details until you have at least a rudimentary visual image. An alternative method is to imagine that you are looking at a mirror or a video image of yourself. This may take practice, though I would note that at this point perfection is not necessary. Just knowing that the image you see is an image of yourself will be enough for now.
- **Adjust the image into one of a self who *has already* met a particular basic need.** Work with just one of the basic needs you identified in Step 1 (this exercise's first bullet point), and allow your self-image to reflect the opposite of that need, as identified in Step 2. Keep the image confined to an image of yourself—background details are not necessary at this stage. Think about how this person that you see, who has already resolved this particular

issue, who has already developed the resources necessary to satisfy this particular basic need, will look. What is his or her posture like? Facial expression? How does he or she breathe? What is the skin tone like? Which muscles are relaxed and which are active? Remember that these details will develop and possibly even change with repeated practice. Again, stick with just one basic need for this exercise—you'll be able to address other needs as you repeat the exercise on successive days.

- **Contemplate the image for at least 30 seconds.**
- **Pull the image into the circle with you and draw it into you.** Wear it like clothing; wrap it around you; let it interpenetrate your body and mind. Let your own body, posture, breathing, facial expression, etc., reflect what you saw in this image. Let the memories of this (future) self who has already satisfied this basic need be your memories.
- **Breathe and banish.** Repeat Step 3.
- **Be open to thoughts, epiphanies, and suggestions from your unconscious mind** that may occur throughout the day as a result of this practice.

Of course, if we can do this with prosperity, we can self-create god/dess images for just about any quality. Some traditional pantheons include deities for many different aspects of life and our internal pantheons may be even larger and more inclusive. The following exercise can be practiced as many times as you'd like, for whatever qualities you wish to work with.

Exercise 4.4 Instant God/dess

- **Decide on a quality** that you either have and would like to enhance, or one that you don't have and would like to acquire. For instance, creativity, compassion, patience, strength, assertiveness, financial skill, adaptability, understanding, concentration, flexibility, love, sex appeal, or whatever you decide upon. Make sure this quality is a positive one, that is, one that stands on its own and is not expressed as a lack of something else (for instance, "reduced stress" might be expressed here as "relaxation," "no more bad luck" might be expressed for these purposes as "good luck," and so on).
- **Breathe and banish.**
- **Create a dissociated image of yourself**, standing or sitting. Eliminate background scenery and any accessories, objects, props, and so on that might be in your image so that the image is just you.
- **Begin to adjust the physiology** of the imagined person to include more and more of your desired quality. Pay attention to and adjust facial expression, posture, breathing, movements, skin tone, muscle usage, and anything else that might pertain.
- **Adjust the structure of the image** (submodalities) for greater impact. Experiment with image size, color depth and quality, image

location, and special effects such as glows, sparkles, and shimmers. Take each of these to its greatest intensity—for instance, the image could be increased to much greater than life-size. If this image were a god/dess of that particular quality, how would these submodalities manifest? Just how big is a god/dess of x?

- **Begin to add in extra features and aspects** from other humans, animals, machines as appropriate to a god/dess of this quality. For instance, if cunning and strength are useful to this entity, give it some qualities of a tiger or other animal that might represent those qualities (head, body, teeth, eyes, whatever). If enhanced intelligence or processing speed is important, then maybe a computer chip or having a computer as an accessory might work. Take as much time as is necessary to test out some of these qualities. Notice which ones feel the best and keep them. Have fun with this, and make your image fantastic.
- **Adjust physiology to account for the additions.** If you added a computer chip to the brain, how would that be reflected in facial expression, breathing, posture, etc.?
- **Contemplate the image for at least 30 seconds.**
- **Pull the image into the circle with you and draw it into you.** Wear it like clothing, wrap it around you, let it interpenetrate your body and mind. Let your own body, posture, breathing, facial expression, etc., reflect what you saw in this image. Let the memories of

this (future) self who possesses the quality you would like to enhance be your memories now.

- **Breathe and banish.**
- **Be open to thoughts, epiphanies, and suggestions from your unconscious mind** that may occur throughout the day as a result of this practice.

five

Tingling and Sparkling

Changing Your Brain

The purpose of magick may ultimately be about changing our lives. When we talk about changing ourselves or changing our lives or changing our perception, we are talking, ultimately, about neurological change. Our brains must change if our experience of the world is to change. If we want more woohoo, then we must teach our neurology to organize itself for more woohoo. The kinds of change we want to happen in our brains are *neuroplasticity* and *neurogenesis.* Neuroplasticity is the brain's ability to change neural pathways as it learns. Neurogenesis is the brain's ability to grow entirely new neurons and neural pathways.[1]

There are many ways to encourage both neuroplasticity and neurogenesis. Almost any kind of learning will change neural pathways. Drugs of various kinds encourage growth and change in the brain. For instance, recent genomic research into LSD demonstrated that the chemical activates genes responsible for neuroplasticity.[2] That seems to suggest that psychedelics tap directly into the brain's ability to learn. Some antidepressant drugs activate neurogenesis in the hippocampus (which may be a more important mode of action in the treatment of depression than serotonin uptake inhibition).[3] Movement and exercise promote both neuroplasticity and neurogenesis.[4]

For our purposes, we'll consider three factors of perceptual experience that encourage neuroplasticity and neurogenesis: *intensity*, *duration*, and *novelty*. It's simple enough—if an experience is intense enough, we remember it. How easy is it to recall a particularly intense experience? If an experience lasts long enough, we remember it. How easy is it to recall the things that you do every day of your life? If an experience is new and different enough, we remember it. How easy is it to recall your first kiss, your first rock concert, or your first time driving a car? Intense experiences change us and so do new and different experiences, as does repetition and rehearsal.

Aleister Crowley summarized the technique of invocation as "Enflame thyself with praying," suggesting intensity and duration, at the least.[5]

A ritual or meditation practice that continues over time may partake of all three factors. The discipline of daily practice supplies duration, the change of state created by the practice creates novelty, and continued improvement in concentration and technique can increase intensity. Indeed, brain-imaging studies of experienced meditators demonstrate physical changes in the brain. A 2005 study of experienced practitioners of Vipassana ("insight" or "mindfulness" meditation) conducted at Massachusetts General Hospital, for instance, demonstrated that the practice appeared to encourage neuroplasticity and neurogenesis in areas of the cerebral cortex associated with attention, memory, and integration of emotions. In short, these areas were thicker in experienced Vipassana practitioners than in the non-meditating control group.[6]

There are many ways to add intensity, duration, and novelty to our imaginings. Adjusting submodalities can increase intensity. State entities created from our internal energy flows, if they flow or pulse, suggest duration. And new configurations can create novelty. Ready for a new configuration that explores all of the above?

What happens when our state entities meet our pantheon? Will we find a solemn procession of secret chiefs and internal gurus? Or the party we've always suspected was happening somewhere in the collective unconscious? We've explored the use of dissociated images to create god-like entities and we've practiced the creation of state entities for a variety of purposes. Now we're going to put the pieces together and endow our personal pantheon with abilities, states, and flexibility of behavior.

Exercise 5.1 Instant Empowerment

- **Decide on a quality that you want to work with,** something you want to invoke into your life or that might add woohoo to particular situations.

- **Create a dissociated image of yourself**, in front of you and facing you.
- Tweak the image of yourself to include the desired quality. What would you look like with that quality? How would it affect posture, facial expression, breathing, and other physiological modeling indicators?
- **Make that image god- or goddess-sized.** For most purposes, this will be at least life-sized. Some gods or goddesses may be larger than human size; some may be vast.
- Leaving that image in place, externally, turn your attention back into yourself. **Create an energy flow in your body for that quality** based on the feeling you would have if you were powerfully experiencing that quality. Enhance it by experimenting with size, color, and special effects.
- **Externalize that energy flow as a state entity—and place that state entity inside the god-like dissociated image** previously created.
- **Breathe into this combined creation** and notice how it changes.
- **Contemplate the creation** for at least 30 seconds.
- **Step into the creation** and turn to face the direction that it is facing.
- Take some time to **notice what happens** as you stand in the same place as this entity.
- Keep the entity with you and **walk around your space.**

- **Imagine what it would be like to enter various situations** in your life with this entity enveloping you.
- **Keep as much of the entity and experience with you as you deem appropriate.**

Just as a human being may be able to function well in a variety of states and situations, some gods and goddesses have a range of abilities and powers. This can give the entity a great deal of flexibility to act or offer information in many areas of life. The following exercise explores one of many ways to add powers to your entity.

Exercise 5.2 Adding Powers to Your God/dess

- **Consider a situation in your life in which you may need a variety of resources.** For instance, in a business situation, you might decide that it was important to have patience, perseverance, mathematical acumen, negotiation skills, and so forth. Make a list of at least three qualities.
- **Create an "instant god,"** as in the previous exercise, that reflects the nature of that situation—for instance, a personal god or goddess of business that might fit the situation in the example above.
- Instead of a single state entity applied to the dissociated instant god, **add one state entity for each of the qualities** you listed. That is, in

the one entity called "Business God," we might add state entities representing patience, perseverance, math skills, and so on.

- **Breathe into the god/dess** and pay attention to how these all combine and/or interrelate. Observe any changes.
- **Contemplate the creation** for at least 30 seconds.
- **Step into it, walk around a bit, and imagine what it would be like to enter various situations** in your life with this entity enveloping you.
- **Keep as much of the entity and experience with you as you deem appropriate and absorb anything else.** When you are fully done with the entity, absorb it all back into you and banish with Expansion/Contraction breathing.

In a sense, the process of adding state entities to your god/dess image is much like giving them chakras or a meridian system. Suddenly the image can express quite a bit more information about its state—and can have the flexibility to adapt resources from multiple states and the ability to change states when necessary. The entity becomes a bit more like a human being, with a choice of mind-states to operate from. It also gives us a way to operate on the image, improve it, and empower it (similar to what you might do for yourself) using meditation or energy work to change your state or improve your health. Balance your god's chakras with woohoo!

Symbols and Anchors

We've already discussed how god/dess images, both traditional and meta-magical, are symbols for states. We might choose to differentiate between states that represent a single kind of experience, as symbolized by energy flows and state entities, and states that might include a longer time frame and the flexibility to move through a variety of experiences. In terms of traditional magick, the former might be simpler entities such as servitors, elementals, demons, or angels. The latter, more complex entities, are the deities, the gods and goddesses.

Symbols, of course, are anchors, cues that we can use to re-access states and information. When we see a god/dess figure (or read their name, hear their song, feel their presence, etc.), our brains activate the equivalent states. This is the essence of invocation; being in the presence of the god elicits the qualities within us. Experiencing the states as you create the god anchors them to the image and allows you to re-access the states at will simply by contemplating or visualizing the god/dess.

Anchors can activate your physiology before you are even conscious of the change. If you drive, for instance, hopefully a red light will have your foot moving to the brake without the need to ponder the significance of colored lights. The smell of dinner cooking can make you salivate faster than you can remember what kind of pets Pavlov kept. A telephone ringtone can you make you grab for the phone—or grumble about it—before you realize what you are doing.

Wouldn't it be sweet if our god-consciousnesses could kick in automatically, exactly when needed? Would that add some woohoo to your life story? Intentional anchors can be created to activate states or behaviors based on your situation. The swish pattern is a flexible NLP anchoring technique, often used in habit control, which can be adapted to a wide variety of purposes.[7] In its usual configuration, it uses an associated image—the situation—switched with a dissociated image of the self in a resourceful state. The associated image, from your own point of view, includes the sensory cues that will act as the anchor; the dissociated image activates the mirror neuron system to begin invocation. This may sound complex, but when you explore Exercise 5.3, you'll discover that it's a very simple process. For habit change, one might visualize one's own hand just before it reaches for the cigarette pack and then switch that image for a view of a self who knows how to breathe clean, fresh air and considers health to be woohoo. Beyond therapeutic change, the swish can be used to help install positive habits. Want to become motivated to meditate at a certain time or place? Or how about feeling inspired to work on your novel every time you get near your computer?

Using gods and goddesses in the swish pattern can create even more powerful, flexible resource states. Imagine walking into a job interview with god-like powers of rapport. Or cooking dinner with the creativity and finesse of the Goddess of Art, driving your car with the quickness and fluidity of Mercury, or learning magick as the God of Wisdom.

Or, perhaps, filling every nook and cranny of your life's story with woohoo.

Exercise 5.3 Swish Pattern of the Gods

- **Create an empowered god/dess** using one of the techniques already described, but do not step into it—keep it external **and send it off into the distance**, perhaps to the other side of the room.
- **Consider a situation in your life where the qualities of this entity will be useful to you.**
- **Make an image in front of you of how it would look to enter that situation.** Note that this is an associated image, viewed from your own point of view. Place this image close to you, between you and the god/dess, so that it blocks your view of the god.
- As quickly as you can, within the space of a second, if you can manage it, **switch these two images**, sending the associated image (of the situation) off into the distance and bringing the god/dess up close to you.
- Again, as quickly as you can, set the images up with the god in the distance and associated image close to you, then **switch them again**, as quickly as possible. **Repeat this switch as fast as you can, at least three or four times.**
- Then, without consciously thinking about the above procedure, **think about the upcoming situation and notice what happens.**
- **Absorb** any externalized creations back into you.

six

Stepping In

Godforms

The traditional magical practice of assumption of godforms can be a potent, yet extremely time-consuming practice. One of the more common methods, to be practiced over days, weeks, months, or years, goes something like this:

- Find an image of the deity to be invoked. Sit or stand in the posture of the deity and imagine that you look, sound, and feel like the god—that you are the god.
- Study the deity and the pantheon of which it is a part. Learn its story and all the things that the god does, says, owns, and believes.

- Build a small image of the god in your heart. Expand the image until it is as large, or larger than, you.[1]

This is a solid method, based upon a traditional idea that the best representations of the forces within us exist external to us in books of ancient lore and wisdom. Alternatively, some systems stress stepping into the godform, rather than building it up inside you. Variations exist in which god names are vibrated through the body and sigils for the entity are placed in the heart, but the basic idea of filling oneself with aspects of the god remains the same. The same processes can be applied to the personal entities that we create from our own memories, feelings, ideals, and stories.

We already have some of the components. In our system, the forms of entities are built upon the structure of our own mirror neurons, on the model of consciousness that we use to understand our own mind and that of others. The aspects, deeds, beliefs, behavior, and states of the entities can be found in our own perceptual tendencies and imagination, which may take some study and research, but rarely requires books of ancient lore. (There are excellent reasons for working with traditional entities, but that's a different book. They can bring you woohoo, and you can bring woohoo to them, too.)

You may also note some similarity between the "building up" or "stepping in" methods and the swish pattern. In the first instance, even though the god-image is built inside you, it still qualifies as a dissociated image, which is then enlarged to replace the associated experience of yourself in the present. The "stepping in" version is much like the distance-based swish that we explored in the last chapter, except that we move ourselves rather than the images.

Some classical magicians have noted that these techniques can induce powerful physiological responses.[2] Remember that the mirror neurons are also part of the motor neuron system. By imagining the experience of being someone else, gods and goddesses included, we may expect some measure of change in obvious ways such as posture, gestures, quality of voice, and so on, which all may be conscious or unconscious forms of mimicry. More subtle responses can also be detected if we have the subtlety to detect them.

Ideomotor Response

One class of response that may assist us here is that of *ideomotor response* (IMR). An ideomotor response would be when a thought of some kind produces a possibly unconscious muscular response. In hypnosis, IMR is used to set up phenomena such as finger signaling and arm levitation, which can be used to communicate with a subject on an unconscious level. More commonly, IMR is responsible for the kinds of unconscious movement we might describe as facial expression and body language. For the most part, body language is fairly obvious: joy can make us smile or laugh; fear can cause shallow breathing or crying, among other things; love can cause smiling, sighing, or arousal. Some researchers have suggested that IMR is a mirror neuron phenomenon.[3] Ideomotor movements in response to thoughts or to the words or actions of others may be part of a system of communication that we use that influences each others' mirror neurons, outside of awareness.

We may notice IMR when our godform experiments induce it and, if we set it up in advance, we can use these movements as a means of testing and communication. The following exercises are simple and fairly well-known examples of IMR testing. Basic Energy Testing, under a variety of names, is used by a wide range of alternative health practitioners to test for food and substance sensitivities, various biological and metaphysical imbalances, and much more. For our purposes, we'll use IMR testing to communicate with the parts of neurology and physiology that operate within the magical processes of invocation.

Exercise 6.1 Basic Energy Testing

(Requires two people)

- **Person A stands with one arm outstretched directly to one side,** palm down, at the level of the shoulder, relaxed, but maintaining the position. Person B places one hand on A's opposite shoulder, and then rests two fingers lightly just above the wrist of A's outstretched hand.
- **B first calibrates,** determining how strong A's arm is in that position, by exerting a small amount of pressure with his or her two fingers on A's arm. Note that this is not a test of strength or a contest, it is a means of simply testing how much force is necessary to move the arm.
- **A then makes a statement that is obviously true,** for instance "My name is..." and his or her name. **B then tests the arm.**
- **A then makes a statement that is obviously false,** for instance, "My name is..." someone else's name. **B then tests the arm.**

- **Partners then switch roles** and repeat the exercise.
- **Both partners take a few moments to reflect and discuss their experiences.**

Exercise 6.2 Body Pendulum
(This is a solo means of testing.)

- **Stand with feet about hip-width apart, toes facing forward,** in a stable and balanced position.
- **Make a statement that is obviously true** and notice how your balance is affected, whether you are leaning slightly forward or slightly back. These may be very subtle motions and may require you, at first, to wait a few seconds for the response or to repeat the statement until the response becomes noticeable.
- **Make a statement that is obviously false** and notice how your balance is affected.
- **Take a few moments to reflect on what you have experienced.**

As these methods may give varying results in different states of consciousness, it is advisable to recalibrate for each usage. This can be as simple as asking one yes and one no question to determine arm strength for the one method or balance directions for the second. We're going to apply ideomotor response to our magical pursuits, and it's worth at least a mention of how useful it can be to communicate with your neurology in a wide variety of contexts. Use your imagination and figure out all the different ways you can ask how to add more woohoo to your life.

Stepping In

To delve into the godform process a bit deeper, we can use ideomotor testing to evaluate some of the components, particularly those that might involve the mirror neuron system. Some of what we experience when exploring deities both personal and traditional may not actually depend on divinity; imaginary humans have woohoo, too. How do we respond to the human shape of our imagined entities? Step into the next two exercises and find out.

Exercise 6.3 Stepping In #1

- **Calibrate by making true/false statements about your name.** Say "My name is…" and your name, then **test using one of the above methods** (if you use Energy Testing, have someone help you). Then say "My name is…" and someone else's name and test.
- **Create an image of someone you admire,** standing a couple paces away from you.
- **Step into that image and then test statements about names.** "My name is…" and your own name. "My name is…" and the name of the person you admire.
- **Step back out of the image and test again.**

✧✧✧

Exercise 6.4 Stepping In #2

- **Calibrate by testing statements about names,** as above.
- **Have someone else create an image of someone they admire.**
- **Step into the place where he or she has made the image and test statements** about your name and about the name of the person your partner imagined. There are various ways to attempt some measure of experimental control for both "stepping in" exercises, including not saying the names out loud and having your partner think the name of the person he or she admires when you say "My name is…"
- **Step back out of the image and test again.**

In Stepping In #2, the quality of admiration can be substituted with many other qualities, as long as some emotional charge is present. Strong emotions can offer an easily observed range of ideomotor responses in addition to those that we make use of in the tests. Indeed, emotions with more noticeable physical responses, such as fear, joy, hate, love, and lust may serve even better than admiration.

Again, there are some interesting applications for these exercises that can provide woohoo, if you use your imagination. For now, though, the point is simply to note what connections we might find between our imaginings, mirror neurons, and physiology. As with all these experiments, please draw your own conclusions. What happens may be very different from one person to the next—the point is simply to notice what happens for you.

Embodied Metaphor

Mirror neurons appear to be directly connected with our motor functions—and they also appear to be an important part of whatever process allows us to use metaphor.[4] Quite a bit of the metaphor commonly found in conversational and written language can be described as *embodied*.[5] That is, the metaphor refers to the human body, or parts thereof. Thus, the idea transmitted by the metaphor can reach [its arm] directly to the mirror neurons where it can [extend a finger to] flip the switch on motor functions, which [use a foot, soccer-style to] kick the body into action. The body [uses its long, beautiful fingers and] spreads out an array of feelings and ideomotor responses, and the mind [suddenly grows a pair of hands and] engages in model-building activities, accessing states and memories that [put on their shoes and] depart before our conscious awareness can [run them down, grab them, and] intercept them. This allows us to make meaning of the metaphor and the communication.

From a magical perspective, it's like there are a lot of little entities [with strong legs and clever hands] running around inside our language. Got it? Metaphor, mirror neurons, and motor functions are all having a party together, all the time. Our magical deities can be considered as macro-metaphors, as deliberately complete, embodied metaphors for aspects of mind and the universe around us.

So what happens when we now perform ideomotor testing with an imagined human figure pumped full of metaphor and woohoo to the point of godhood?

Exercise 6.5 Stepping Into Godforms/Having them Step Into You

- Using one of the methods we have explored previously, **create a god or goddess image.**
- **Step into the god/dess image.**
- **Use ideomotor testing to ask yes/no questions of your entity.** Learn whatever you think might be appropriate to learn from this entity, based on the original qualities and intent used to create the god/dess image.
- **Absorb the entity into you** in whatever way you find appropriate.
- **Create another god/dess image,** of the same entity or a different entity.
- This time, **have the entity step into you.**
- **Use ideomotor testing to ask yes/no questions** and derive whatever information you deem appropriate.
- **Absorb the entity into you** in whatever way you find appropriate.
- **Take a few moments to reflect** on any differences you noted between stepping into an entity and having an entity step into you.

seven

Elementary Ritual

The Ritual Frame

In some systems of magick, the work is conducted within a consecrated circle. The circle is, almost literally, a frame that defines the ritual. Everything within the circle is part of the ritual—outside it's still just your spare room. Certain behaviors also mark off the time when a ritual happens; you step in and out of the circle, the ritual has an opening and closing, or the invocation ends when a particular goal is reached. The simplest ritual frame starts with the decision to begin and stops with the decision to end.

We encounter ritual frames every day. Ritualizing seems to be a fundamental human behavior, something we use and experience in many aspects of our lives. For instance,

instance, if you choose to have a romantic dinner with someone special, the ritual is simply to ensure that every aspect of the situation is aligned with the goal: the lights are dimmed, the candles lit, the champagne chilled, the food perfect, the music soft and suggestive. If you manage to arrange the circumstances for maximum woohoo, then an altered state is produced—a comfortable sharing, excitement, or erotic feeling—and your desired outcome of romance is achieved. This ritual can be repeated with variations to achieve a romantic effect time after time.

Similarly, most of us have rituals that we use to prepare for a day of work, a night out with friends, a shower, or a sneeze. These are all delineated by space, time, behavior, and even state. The sneezing ritual might require fast hands and proximity to Kleenex; it might be over in just a moment, but it is a goal-directed ritual nonetheless, invoking qualities of health, safety, and cleanliness. The sneeze itself is just a reflex action and doesn't quite rise to the level of ritual without the frame that is applied by covering the mouth, using a tissue, cleaning up, and perhaps saying thank you for the ritual "gesundheit" or "god bless you" offered by someone nearby. The frame aligns behaviors toward the goal. Each of these actions is elicited as a kind of anchored response. The first tickle in the nose and you look around for the tissue box, and so on. The ultimate outcome is the state of feeling well.

For the most part, magical ritual can be described as a sequence of anchors enacted within a frame. An anchor may be a word, a gesture, an object, a symbol, or any other ritual component. Information is attached to the anchors through a process of practice, preparation, and study.

Consider a ritual commonly practiced by ceremonial magicians, the Lesser Banishing Ritual of the Pentagram.[1] Ritual anchors include a circle, crosses, pentagrams, a hexagram, gestures, names, and Hebrew words. Imagined geometric figures will convey submodality information—a bright, blue pentagram three feet tall at arm's distance away will influence state differently than a dim, red pentagram that is way across the room. In addition to that information, the student is encouraged to anchor meaning to the geometric figures, movements, and words by study and by practice; esoteric information becomes associated to the symbol along with the state information. Hebrew words, acronyms, and names are used throughout the ritual—and serve remarkably well as anchors as they are otherwise free of meaning to a non-Hebrew-speaking practitioner. These anchors and anchors-to-other-anchors form a shape and sequence that also conveys state information. Each anchor reinforces the next. The ritual helps to establish a mind-state that is conducive to further practice of magick.[2]

Wholeness

What bit of woohoo turns a complex of anchors into a mind-state? One important factor is the idea of *wholeness*. Just as the mirror neurons use various visual, auditory, and kinesthetic cues to identify something as an entity, the brain's theory of mind functions recognize patterns of information that reflect the whole. Our minds operate on the world through a map or model that is as complete as possible, holding as much as we can possibly know through our experience, thoughts, and education about the world. While the emphasis of that map might change as our consciousness shifts through different states and mind-states, each of those maps still, as much as possible, reflects our universe at the moment. In effect, that map is also a map of our consciousness at the moment, a model of our mind-state. It is the job of the theory of mind functions to recognize the difference between random fragments of information and a more-or-less complete map.

Let's sum this up in a simple way: Our minds create an ever-evolving map of the universe at large. The minds of the entities that we create within our minds have their own holistic map. Like Russian dolls, each entity within an entity has a smaller, more simplified map. Thus, the lover that you dream about—a representation of a mind within your own mind, created via mirror neurons and theory of mind functions—probably has a slightly more limited or different range of choices than you do (or the actual person he or she is based upon).

As the entities get smaller and simpler, the symbols of the map become more generalized. At the most generalized level, a symbol for the whole can be created that has a single component—the encompassing circle that we use in ritual, perhaps. The next tiny step toward complexity might jump to two components. We have these symbols in almost every culture: the circle divided into the yin/yang symbol, the two triangles of the hexagram, the Rose Cross, and the binary one/zero. As we begin to add complexity, the number of symbols can increase. We may jump to the four elements of Western esotericism: earth, air, fire, and water; or add spirit for the five elements of the pentagram; or the five elements of Chinese tradition: earth, air, wood, metal, and water; the ten sephiroth of the Qabala; the twelve signs of the zodiac; the sixty-four hexagrams of the *I Ching*; the seventy-eight cards of the Tarot; the over 600,000 words of the English language; and so on. Each of these represent a map or model of the human mind, as well as the universe reflected in it. The symbols become more and more specific, the world divided into discrete qualities as they become more numerous. Short of the actual universe itself, if we can ever fully know such a thing, the most complex mind-state model that we generate is composed of the millions of perceptions, representations, and memories that we have of our world.

For practical purposes, when working with our meta-magical deities, we can choose to represent them with a limited number of generalized elements. These can be chosen consciously and deliberately, based on any theory or practice of world-modeling, such as those listed above. Or the elements can be selected through a process of feedback and revelation, using entities and parts of entities as model-generating tools.

Exercise 7.1 Identifying Elements

- **Choose a major life goal to work with.** What is something in your life toward which you put large amounts of attention and energy?
- **Create a state entity** from the (imagined) feeling of having attained this life goal.
- Communicate with the entity and **ask it to give you a short list of the most important qualities that are necessary for this life goal** to be attained.
- **Write this list down.**
- Thank the state entity and **absorb it back into you.**

✧✧✧

While it may not reflect the entire world in a balanced way, this list of qualities symbolizes everything necessary to attain that goal, a micro-microcosm, if you will, with a narrow focus. This list can now be used as the elements of a ritual, and there are many ways to apply them. One simple choice, as explored in the following exercise, is to create an entity for each element and then arrange them in a geometric shape in relation to where you sit or stand. These can be state entities or full-blown deities that contain any number of state entities.

Exercise 7.2 Magical Entourage

- **Create a dissociated god/dess image for each one of the elements revealed in the "Identifying Elements" exercise.** Create these using the methods explored in previous exercises: Start with a dissociated image of yourself, tweak it to have properties associated with the particular quality, develop a state entity for the quality, and place it into the dissociated image.
- When you have created one god/dess for each of your elements, **arrange them in a shape around you.** Ask them to accompany you on a walk.
- **Take a walk with these god/desses as your magical entourage.** Notice how it feels to move with them accompanying you.
- As you walk, **imagine that you are walking into various situations in your life with these entities protecting or supporting you.** Notice how you feel, imagine, or talk to yourself about these situations.

- Thank the entities and **absorb them back into you.**

In addition to experimenting with the complexity of the entities involved, you can also experiment with the number of elements and ways to arrange them. Do different ritual qualities seem to work better with different shapes? Is there a particular general arrangement that works for most of your rituals, or do the shapes need to be unique for each one?

Different schools of magick sometimes have characteristic ritual structures. For instance, there's a configuration that's found in the Lesser Banishing Ritual of the Pentagram, as well as many pentagram and hexagram rituals that lets you know it comes from the body of work associated with the Golden Dawn tradition. Many of Aleister Crowley's Thelemic rituals also used a very similar structure.[3]

The Lesser Banishing Ritual of the Pentagram uses entities and concepts that are arrayed upon a symbolic map of the four elements: earth, air, fire, and water. It is quite literally a map, with elements attributed to the compass points and a geometric form that the magician can explore by turning or walking around within the circle. When the magician has explored every quarter and contacted each entity, the result is a unique, ritual-induced mind-state.

If we borrow some bits and pieces from that particular ritual and use them with our self-generated symbolism and content, we take our Meta-Magick a step closer to full-fledged ritual work.

Exercise 7.3 Lesser Banishing Ritual of the Entities

- **Imagine a circle around you.** Clear it with Expansion/Contraction breathing.
- Using the elemental qualities identified in the preceding exercises or an entirely new set of elements created by the same methods, **create a set of god/desses and place them as symmetrically as possible just outside your circle.**
- One at a time, **ask each entity to project its quality through the circle**, filling the circle and yourself with that quality. Note if this projected quality has color, sound, feeling, taste, or smell associated with it. Let each entity fully project its quality and then finish before moving to the next entity.
- **Create an energy flow in yourself that represents a powerful resource state.** Adjust the submodalities of that energy flow until it is exceptionally powerful.
- **Express the feeling of that energy flow as a sound and a gesture.** Repeat the sound and gesture several times.
- Thank each entity (and yourself!), then **absorb all entities and imaginings back into yourself.**
- **Pay attention** to any feelings or thoughts that you may experience as a result of this operation.

✧✧✧

There are no limits to the variety of rituals we can create like this and an equally infinite number of ways to apply them. The kind of Meta-Magick we've been experimenting with is designed to give you some understanding of how our minds work when we are performing invocation. With that understanding in hand, you have the means to apply magick to all kinds of woohoo with your own self-designed rituals.

Exercise 7.4 Bonus Exercise

- **Create your own ritual structure using multiple god/desses.** Factors which you can experiment with include elements, complexity of entities, sequence of entities, location of entities, whether entities project qualities or draw them in, whether you step into the entity or it steps into you, which ritual participants (you and the entities) are in motion and which are not, use of gestures and other anchors—and any other factors that strike your magical or aesthetic fancy.

eight

The Mastery Technique

Developing Mastery

Again, the ritual elements that we have explored so far can be combined and recombined in an almost infinite number of ways. The Mastery Technique is an example of how your own feelings, memories, and behavioral tendencies can be used to create a complete and moderately complex magical ritual. The technique may be practiced daily, indefinitely, or until you are satisfied with the woohoo. Allow for a learning curve. The first time you attempt this it may require an hour or more to complete all the elements. You may also choose to practice it in increments, and build up your resources and abilities over a period of days until you are performing the entire operation. Whichever you choose, when you become proficient this may take no longer than 10 or 15 minutes to perform. It seems complex at first, but as you practice you'll find it easier and easier to remember the various elements of the exercise.

Exercise 8.1A Developing Resources

1. **Select six qualities or behaviors that are components of your highest aspiration.** These may be chosen by an entity of your choice, or can be consciously decided upon. You may select qualities that you already have, strongly. You may select qualities that you are weak in and hope to develop. You may select qualities that you do not have and hope to acquire. These could be chosen from a field of qualities that includes, but is not limited to, confidence, compassion, strength, intelligence, decisiveness, motivation, joy, sexiness, directness, extroversion, introversion, creativity, passion, leadership, intuition, spirituality, and rapport. Select only qualities that contribute to your highest aspiration, to your ultimate purpose and function on Planet Earth. At this point, your highest aspiration may be something vague that you refer to as "highest aspiration;" or it may be something very well-defined that you refer to by a term you already know. For each of the six qualities that you have selected, develop a movement or gesture by the following process.
2. **Sitting or standing, recall a time when you had a powerful experience of the chosen**

quality. If you are working with a quality with which you have limited or no direct experience, something you want to strengthen or acquire, then you may select another person that you know who has this quality at times and imagine what it would be like to be that person at those times.

3. **Remember or imagine the visual components of this experience:** what colors were in your field of vision, whether you could see movement or stillness, whether it was light or dark, and anything else you can recall.
4. **As you notice what you saw, remember or imagine what you heard** during this experience: sounds or silence, voices or tones, rhythms or noises, background sounds, and anything else you may have been able to hear.
5. **As you notice what you saw and heard, remember or imagine what you felt** during this experience: notice where in your body the feeling begins and where it moves to as the feeling develops. Notice what kind of feeling it may be, pressure, temperature, movement, texture, or whatever it was that you felt.
6. **Give the feeling a color or colors.** "If this feeling were a color, what would it be?" Apply the color to wherever you feel the feeling so that you end up with a colored map of the sensation in your body.
7. **Make the color brighter, richer, more vibrant, or whatever also makes the feeling more intense.** For most people and most

feelings, making the color brighter or more vibrant will increase the feeling, although for some people and some feelings making the color more muted or dimmer will increase the feeling. Use what works for you. Intensify the experience to exhilaration.

8. **Breathe deeply and make or imagine the color flowing through more and more of your body.**
9. **Feel how the feeling has intensified.** Savor it.
10. **Take a deep breath and then express the feeling as a gesture or movement.** Take note of this movement in some form that will enable you to remember it later.
11. **Repeat for each of your six chosen qualities** so that you develop a catalog of six movements that you can use in part two (below). These same six movements will serve you through many repetitions of The Mastery Technique. If you ever decide that you want to change, tweak, or empower your work, you can return to this section and create new movements based on the same or alternative qualities.

Exercise 8.1B The Mastery Technique

1. **Imagine a circle drawn on the floor around you.** Make the circle about twice the diameter of your outstretched arms or as close to that size as space permits.

2. **Perform at least three cycles of Expansion and Contraction Breathing** in the circle.
3. **In your mind, notice six points along the circumference of the circle,** spaced equal distances apart.
4. **Walk to the edge of your circle and pace around the circumference. As you get to each of the six points, perform one of the movements** that you created in Developing Resources, as fully and completely as possible. Do this until you have performed all six of your movements, one at each of the six, equidistant points.
5. **Return to the center of the circle.**
6. **Face one of the six points. Imagine seeing yourself standing at the circumference of the circle, performing the movement that you performed there.**
7. **Take a Full Breath. As you exhale, using the entire breath, say the name of the quality** that applies to the movement and point you are looking at. At the same time, **imagine that a color or energy or vibration or sound or feeling is emanating from that image of you.** Allow that color or whatever to fill the entire circle.
8. **Take a moment to experience what that color or energy feels like** as you stand in a circle full of it.
9. **Repeat for each of the six points/ movements.**

10. **Take a moment to see all the self-images and movements at the same time, along the circumference of the circle.**
11. **Take a large step backward.**
12. **Imagine the six movement-images of yourself, either one at a time or all at once, whichever is easiest for you, moving into the center of the circle,** just in front of you.
13. **Allow them to combine** in whatever way they seem predisposed to. They may take a definite shape or become amorphous. They may still be recognizable as images of you, or they may not. However it happens is fine.
14. **Take Full Breaths and use your exhalations to send attention and energy into the shape** for at least one minute.
15. **Optional: In your mind you may now communicate with this shape/entity.** Ask it what it would like to be called and how to call it back again faster and more powerfully. Ask it what you can learn from it concerning your highest aspirations in life or what it can tell you about changes, additions, and deletions in your behavior and life in general that can bring you closer to your goals. And anything else that might occur to you to ask it, as long as you remain focused on your highest aspirations and goals.
16. **Step forward, into the shape/entity.**

17. **Take a moment to appreciate and enjoy the experience.** Notice how you feel, what you hear, what you see, and anything else that presents itself to consciousness.

18. **Breathe and absorb all your imaginings back into you,** except the circle.

19. **Take at least three Expansion and Contraction Breaths.**

20. **Absorb the circle back into you.**

21. **Be open to thoughts, epiphanies, and suggestions from your unconscious mind** that may occur throughout the day as a result of this practice.

nine

The Time Axis

Timelines

We represent our experience of time through sensory metaphor, just as we do most other experiences. The simplest and most common of these representations is a linear metaphor, a timeline. Linear time is expressed through language such as "the future is ahead of us," and "the past is left behind." Research has demonstrated that we respond physiologically to these representations, as we do with other embodied metaphors. In a study that used motion sensors, researchers discovered that experimental subjects tend to sway forward when thinking about the future and tend to lean backward when thinking about the past.[1] Other cultures, it may be noted, have alternatives to the ahead/

behind metaphor that we favor. For instance, the Aymara people of South America typically represent the past as ahead and the future behind.[2] We also express linear time through cause-effect relationships that may have their basis in language more than in the fractal complexity of the world around us.

> *Deeper yet, we encounter the idea that the structure of language itself, the grammar and syntax of the words, defines our perception of reality. Our language presupposes a variety of things about the linearity of time ("I went to the store* before *coming home."), about cause and effect ("The cars hit* because *Fred ran the red light."), and about the nature of being ("Socrates is a man."). In these examples, "before" presupposes linearity (as do most, if not all, time-related words), "because" suggests a chain of actions followed by consequences (when, in fact, Fred's running of the red light might have been equally complicit in causing the accident with the speed of the other motorist, the exact timing of Fred's arrival in the intersection, and the many situations that may have influenced his timing), and "is" creates identity (while Socrates might exhibit manly qualities, he "is" also a philosopher, a wearer of togas, a drinker of wine, etc.). If our language structured grammar and syntax differently, our conceptions of time, causality, and being might be extremely different.*[3]

Like the other simple geometric figures we use to express concepts in ritual, the timeline can be used to express, explore, and work with our states. As a therapeutic modality, timeline therapy was originally developed by NLP cofounder Richard Bandler and was further explored by Tad James, Wyatt Woodsmall, Steve and Connierae Andreas, and many others.[4] The method given here is a simplified one, modified to fit our magical, rather than therapeutic, purpose.

Exercise 9.1 Finding a Timeline

- **Select some activity that you do on a regular basis** that happens in a similar state each time. This could be a ritual or meditation practice, for instance, or could be something as simple as washing the dishes, brushing your teeth, or taking a shower.
- **Remember when you most recently performed the behavior. Remember some time a day or two in the past when you did it. Remember when you performed the behavior a week, a month, and a year ago. Think about what it will be like to do this thing tomorrow, the next day, the coming week, in a month, or a year.**
- Notice how you represent these memories to yourself. In particular, pay attention to the submodality of location in each sense that is experienced. **Notice where you place these memories.** (And, once again, this is about form rather than content. "In front of me, off to the left about three feet." is a preferable answer to "In my bathroom.")
- **If you were to draw a line between these locations, which way would point to the future?** Which way to the past? If they seem to need help lining up, ask yourself "what if they were on a line?" Imagine that they are.

For many people, this exercise will elicit a fairly linear sequence of experiences. These tend to be slanted, curved, or set at a slight angle. The line drawn between the locations may run from left to right in front of you, or it may tend more toward a forward/backward arrangement. Timelines may be more useful for the following experiments when, through curve, angle, or position, they allow each of the memories to be seen from your position in the "present." For instance, with a line that is level and runs directly forward and back, memories may block each other from view and only the closest examples may be readily accessed. Or if the closer representations are huge, they may also block the metaphoric view of the other memories. These kinds of experiences may be expressed in language; for example, "I just can't see past that time when x did y," "Everything went downhill from that point on," or "In later years we just lost sight of those things." More useful and woohooful metaphors might include "Her future lay before her," "Your future is looking up," or "Have one foot in the future." Since this is your own mind and your metaphor for the chronology of your own life, you can arrange it any way you please, so adjustments to your timeline for ease of experiment are encouraged. Be in the present, with full awareness of your history and where the future may take you.

There are all kinds of fun things you can do once you have established the basic timeline metaphor. In the therapeutic context, the time line is used to carry resources into past and future. That's a useful approach in the magical context, too. The timeline can be used to let your invocations transcend the present and carry woohoo to your past and future selves, as in the following two exercises.

Exercise 9.2 Energetic Slide

- **Elicit a timeline for an ongoing aspect of your life** that you would like to improve. If you are concerned about a relationship, a business situation, or a long-term creative project, for example, then find a series of memories and future projections for that situation. Find a useful timeline for them, using the methods mentioned previously.
- **Create an energy flow for a powerful, positive, resourceful state.** Enhance the energy flow until it is so full of woohoo that physiological responses of all kinds make you feel wonderfully powerful, positive, and resourceful.
- With the enhanced energy flow in you, **walk along your timeline,** taking the state of the energy flow with you into the past and into the future. Make sure that you walk into and through any particular memories or projections that can benefit from this state.
- Return to the present and think about the immediate future of the situation in question. **Notice any changes that have occurred** in your thoughts about this aspect of your life.

To add more woohoo to the equation, we can expand this exercise to include a full-tilt god/dess.

Exercise 9.3 Walking God/dess

- **Create a god/dess by any of the means previously explored.**
- **Step into the god/dess and walk along your timeline,** taking the visualizations and states of the entity with you into the past and future. As the god/dess, walk into and through the memories and projections that can most benefit from this state.
- Return to the present. **Notice any changes that have occurred** in your thoughts and behavior concerning this aspect of your life.

Entity Time

The line is a simple metaphor for the complex phenomena of time; other and more complex representations may convey different or more information. Even our natural, unadjusted representations of time, when we explore them enough, turn out to be somewhat non-linear. Most people seem to have multiple timelines. In different states, the memories are accessed in various ways and lines emerge in different spatial locations and configurations. Some people have lines that are decidedly non-linear to begin with; they loop and swirl, spiral, and branch off in unusual ways. These shapes themselves may change as their owners experience different states.

Not only can our states have unique timelines, each entity that forms in our neurons will have its own timeline or timelines. Every god or goddess has its legend, the tale of its origins, life, deeds, death, and, sometimes, life after death or resurrection. The following exercise may require a little more time and imagination than the previous ones. You may also wish to have writing or recording materials on hand, in case the information gets to be too much or too detailed to remember.

Exercise 9.4 Timeline of the Gods

- **Create a god/dess** using one of the methods previously described. Make it wonderful and full of woohoo.
- **Ask the entity to elicit its own timeline** as if it were a truly autonomous being. That is, we're not looking for the timeline that starts "You created me five minutes ago...," but rather the one that describes the metaphoric or mythic origins and life story of the god/dess. The entity may be able to create the timeline itself with minimal suggestion, or you may have to guide it through the steps of eliciting memories and future projections, noting the submodalities of location and size, and drawing a line between them to create the timeline. At this point, only the god/dess needs to know all the details of the timeline—if you can be aware of it in some general form, that is sufficient.
- Have the god/dess move along the timeline from beginning to end, pausing at regular intervals to describe to you where it is and what it is doing (in its memories and projections). Follow along and **elicit the story, the biography of god/dess.**

- **Remember or record this story** in whatever is best for you.
- **Thank and reabsorb the god/dess** and its timeline.
- **Contemplate the story** of the god/dess and note whatever lessons, useful metaphors, or epiphanies might come to mind as a result.

ten

Shaping the Cloud

Chronology and Self

Just as every state has some element of duration, every story has a component of time. Some stories have linear narratives that take you from beginning to end in a straight line. Some move generally in one direction but jump over irrelevant periods. Some stories may be told through multiple points of view that run through time parallel to each other. Some are told through backstory, through unpredictable jaunts forward and backward in time, and even through entirely random sequences. While human life is usually represented as a straight line from birth to death, our minds rarely operate in a linear fashion. We respond to the movies, stories, and novels that are told in flashbacks, foreshadowing, and parallel story lines because that's how our minds often organize our own memories and experiences.

The straight line state of mind may be an artifact of language and the metaphors that we use. The associations that we use to recall memories often have more to do with state than chronology. The feeling of a state can initiate transderivational search, flipping through a range of memories with the same feeling. When someone feels sad, everything they remember is a bummer, and when someone feels joy, everything they remember about life is good. The same holds true for other kinds of anchors; for instance, the smell of apple pie may bring up memories of childhood or mom or favorite desserts of the past decade. It may be that only after we retrieve a memory via association do we apply the linear structures, much the way we might piece together the chronology of a fictional mystery only after enough clues have been revealed.

And the solution to that mystery is ... ourselves. Outside of conscious awareness, the brain somehow manages to pull all kinds of wonderful story elements from the fractal complexity of our ongoing experience. Chronology. Plot. Characters, including that principal character, the self. These are all constructs, creations, beliefs that we make about who we are; self-created meaning applied to ... self.

The sense of self assures us that we are the same person from moment to moment, that there is a continuity of something that we identify as "self." A network of structures in the right frontoparietal area of the brain appears to account for the identification of "self" in the present moment.[1] When this area is damaged, anesthetized, or disrupted with a magnetic beam, subjects are unable to recognize their own face in a mirror and may not recognize their own limbs as belonging to themselves. Normally, the brain continues to identify "me" even though it might be an angry me, a bold me, a shy me, a me who hasn't yet had his or her morning coffee, or a me on a woohoo-saturated adventure. Behavior and experience may be totally different, yet we still "know" who we are—unless somehow that area of the brain is shut down.

Of course, that part of the brain participates in the dance of information between the mirror neurons and the default network. Just as we make judgments about memories of every kind, we also apply a similar yardstick to the internal representations we make of ourselves. In fact, every memory includes ourselves and the submodality information that modifies the form of that memory tells us something about who we were then. The "self spot" in the brain applies the "me" to the memory regardless of what state, actions, knowledge, and entities were in ascendance at that time. When we get past that illusion of "me," however, we may find that the starring role in the tale was performed by a cast of actors, with a large supporting cast of internal entities representing friends, family, acquaintances, and everyone else who plays a part. And along with the "real" people in our memories, many supporting roles are played by imaginary entities, from the tiny embodied metaphors of our language, to the big, culturally based memetic entities responsible for religion, politics, ethics, morals, science, and so on. Each one of these internal representations has its own chronology, its own tale, its own life and deeds. And these are all part of us, part of the full-sensory story that we experience as our lives.

Once a memory is moved from short-term memory in the hippocampus to long-term memory throughout the brain, the storage system is not particularly chronological. Older memories may start to lose detail as they become compressed more and more into the implied "brain language" of submodality information. They become more vague and the states become more memorable than the content of the experience. You remember how good it felt to be on vacation all those years ago, but perhaps forget the name of the really nice waiter in the restaurant or the color of his eyes. Older memories can be brought back into short-term memory and revived at any time via memory reconsolidation. Aside from the differences in how older memories are stored, the memories are organized by association. Timelines and other metaphors for time seem to be a way of sorting through all of this stored experience and thought, useful structures for bringing memories into conscious awareness.

The Cloud

As the matrix within which we can find timelines and other chronological metaphors, think of our memories, including all our accumulated knowledge, experience, skills, preferences, and tendencies, as a cloud-like array. For many people, this is a fairly random formation and the associations made between one memory and the next are likewise based on the happenstance of state. Alternatively, magical and metaphysical traditions often seek to sort these perceptions and experiences into consciously created categories, providing an overall structure and shape for our lives. For instance, in the tradition of Qabala, the world—our collection of experience and knowledge—becomes organized into the shape of the Tree of Life. States are categorized into the ten sephira, and transitions, associations, and combinations of these states are collected onto the paths between them. In traditions of yoga, experience and states are organized via the chakra system. In astrology, the stuff of our lives is arranged on the chart of our planets and signs.

If you notice that the metaphors we use to shape the entirety of our lives are the same variety of elements as those used to shape our internal entities, you get a gold pentagram. Everything we recognize as an entity is based in the same neurocircuitry that makes our own minds. Our world or universe as a whole can be experienced as the largest entity yet, a fractal reiteration of consciousness on a grand scale. Once we are able to recognize the pattern on this larger, higher, deeper (or submodality term of your choice) level, then we can move the bit of consciousness marked "I" (your point of view) through it in any number of ways.

First let's conduct a little experiment to find out how your cloud of perceptions and memory is sorted now.

Exercise 10.1 Cloud Watching

- **Create a list of the most important states in your life.** If you've experimented with the exercises to this point, you'll have some idea of what kinds of things you'll want to work with. You can include states like sleep, meditation, or trance, or states that relate to qualities in your life such as compassion, patience, focus, work, and so on. These can be generalized and the list need not include every single kind of state, just the main ones that help to define your life. This list can be created by asking an entity, as we did when finding elements, or it may already be obvious to you. For this particular exercise, stick with states rather than using a traditional metaphysical system.

- For each state you have listed, **access a range of memories by transderivational search:**
  - **Recall a single experience of a state.**
  - **Pay attention to the feeling** associated with the state.
  - **While experiencing that feeling, let your mind find other memories in which you had a similar feeling.** Notice how these additional memories are accessed—whether they come easily, which senses are involved, what information you can recall that you haven't thought of in a while, and so on.
  - **Notice the location of these memories.** Again, we are thinking about location as a submodality quality, where you place the representation of the memory in your cloud of perceptions. Once a memory is accessed, however briefly (and some may take only a fraction of a second to identify, or may be identified too quickly for conscious awareness), it can be represented to consciousness as a shape, icon, or presence in space—constant awareness of the content is not necessary.
  - **Repeat with the rest of the states on your list.**

- **Notice the overall shape of the cloud.** Remember or record this shape, if possible.

Your cloud may be symmetrical or asymmetrical; it may be regular or irregular; it may have an identifiable geometric shape or it may not. This configuration of memories and experience is as unique to each of us as our retinal pattern or kitchen clutter. Actually, it is probably more like the kitchen clutter; it can be organized and adapted to different configurations and environments. That is, you can change the shape of your cloud at any given time (and, very likely, you already do; you can find out by repeating your cloud watching on different occasions, in different states).

Navigating the Cloud

The cloud is the medium within which the story of your life is stored. A personal narrative is formed by the associations between memories, represented metaphorically by the way you navigate through the cloud. By choosing new ways to move through the cloud, new narratives can be created and resources can be carried from one area of life to another.

In occult Qabala, the magician has a choice of how he or she will explore the sephira, whether the journey starts at the bottom or the top of the tree, whether it moves sequentially, in the numbered order of the spheres, or whether it zigs and zags in different patterns. Likewise, the way that you explore and move through your cloud to identify or create narratives can follow a variety of differently shaped paths. The following exercise explores a method for creating these paths and patterns.

Exercise 10. 2 Cloud Hopping

- **Imagine the shape of your cloud matrix.** If necessary, you can enlarge the shape, blow it up so that it is large enough to walk around in. If such a size is too unwieldy for your space, you can imagine the size and navigation without physically moving.
- **Create a geometric shape within the cloud.** These shapes can be two- or three-dimensional. They can be timelines or they can be figures whose meaning is not known until you explore them. Suggested shapes include circles, squares, triangles, spirals, cubes, and pyramids. Imagine the shape superimposed within your cloud.
- Either physically or imaginatively, **move along the lines of the geometric figure** you have created, experiencing states and memories as you pass through them. The speed you travel may determine the amount of detailed information that you experience as you move through. It is not necessary to consciously retrieve all memories or information; get as much as you feel comfortable with.
- **Notice if new personal narratives occur to you,** new ideas about yourself, or new ideas about your world. Remember or record these.
- **Repeat with different geometric figures.**

✧✧✧

What you carry with you through life, your beliefs, attitudes, presuppositions, skills, and tools, will also change how you respond to the perceptions and situations that you encounter. Just as it was possible to carry a state and/or entity up and down your timeline, you can bring states and resources with you on your journey through your cloud.

Exercise 10.3 Energy Cloud

- **Imagine the shape of your cloud matrix.**
- **Create a geometric figure within it,** as in the previous exercise.
- **Create an energy flow** within your body for a powerful, positive, and resourceful state.
- **Move through the cloud, along the lines of the geometric figure,** experiencing states or memories as you pass through them.
- **Notice if new personal narratives occur to you,** new ideas about yourself, or new ideas about your world. Remember or record these.
- **Repeat with different energy flows and geometric figures.**

Exercise 10.4 God/dess's Choice

- **Imagine the shape of your cloud matrix.**
- **Create a god/dess** by one of the methods explored previously.
- **Ask the god/dess what geometric shape it prefers** to navigate through the cloud.

- **Step into the god/dess.**
- **Create the geometric figure.**
- In the form of the god/dess, **move along the lines of the geometric figure.**
- **Notice if new narratives occur to you,** about your self or about the god/dess, or new ideas about your world. Remember or record these.
- **Repeat with different energy flows and geometric figures.**

While these exercise descriptions are brief, you could literally spend the rest of your life exploring inside your cloud. And, in a sense, that's pretty much what we do, consciously and unconsciously, all day long—although in a somewhat random and haphazard way. We go in and out of states as we encounter anchors within the maps of our environment. The exercises offer guidelines for making conscious and even purposeful explorations.

Cloud Organization

We can decrease the randomness and increase the woohoo by making a few adjustments to the shape and organization of the cloud. Rather than applying a traditional metaphysical system as the organizing principle, we can organize the whole structure of our cloud in the same way we organize other representations of the whole. We can ask an entity for a set of elements, for the factors that make us who we are, and then sort our memories and experiences through the elemental arrangement, as in the following exercise.

Exercise 10.5 Elementary Cloud

- **Select a god/dess** who has toured through your cloud in its present form, as in the God/dess's Choice exercise.
- **Ask the entity what it believes the defining elements of your consciousness may be.** Make a list and remember or record it. This list may be similar to your original collection of states from which you derived the cloud, or it may be very different.
- **Ask the entity what shape to arrange the elements.** Be open to any kind of arrangement. Elements may be distinct or may overlap each other. Elements may be arranged symmetrically or asymmetrically.
- Imagine the new elemental arrangement superimposed over your existing cloud. **Begin to sort memories, ideas, behaviors, and everything else you've got in there into these elemental zones.** Some may be filed in more than one category. This can be accomplished in several ways:
  - Stand or imagine yourself in a zone. Recall or create an experience that relates as purely as possible to that element. Use the Transderivational Memories technique to allow your mind to range through associated experiences. Repeat at least twice for each zone.
  - Ask the god/dess or other entities to sort the experiences for you. Make sure that you observe this in at least symbolic form.

  - Look, listen, or feel the complete shape of your cloud and identify what submodality markers are associated with each element. Memories might be tagged with colors, shapes, words, sounds, or particular feelings. Sort the memories into elemental zones based on these sensory distinctions that you have made in your metaphoric model. For instance, send all the glowing blue ones into the zone for "relaxation," all the dark red ones into the zone for "passion," and so on, depending on your chosen elements and the sensory markers that you have noticed.

- **Notice any thoughts, epiphanies, or new narratives that occur to you.**

Think of these reorganized clouds as experimental efforts—as something that can be modified, changed, or done away with at any time. In fact, it is possible to have a repertoire of different elemental qualities and cloud shapes; you can select the most appropriate one for whatever situation you find yourself in. To do this properly, these cloud structures are best worked out and practiced ahead of time, before they are needed. Each can be recalled with an anchor of some sort, a word, a symbol, or, if it is unique enough, the shape of the cloud arrangement itself.

We can take these shapes and have even more woohoo-ful fun with them by applying some of our submodality knowledge to the totality of the cloud.

Exercise 10. 6 The Silver Lining

- **Imagine the total shape of your cloud,** in whatever arrangement you prefer to work with. See it, feel it, and hear it as a single unified object.
- **Adjust submodalities** for the entirety of the shape. Move the shape into a location that has a lot of woohoo. Make your representation of the cloud bigger, shinier, or more colorful. Add sparkles, glows, diffraction, or whatever increases the good feelings, interest, intrigue, and general level of woohoo.
- **Remember or record this representation.**
- **Notice any thoughts, epiphanies, or changes in your life** as a result of this adjusted shape.

Once you have found a cloud shape that is personally appealing and full of woohoo, you can repeat the Energy Cloud and God/dess's Choice exercises, moving through the newly adjusted cloud to find new associations, ideas, and narratives. But now, of course, it is probably a more definite shape and you may want to call it something other than a cloud. Just as the qabalistic Tree of Life suggests the shape of a tree, perhaps you can find a pattern of wholeness in your former cloud that has an obvious and useful name.

The stories that can be derived from journeys through these "organized" clouds often suggest more in the way of mythic narrative than clouds in their original forms. Hierarchies of states and entities may become apparent. Different stories can emerge depending on which direction you move through the representation, transitioning from one element to the next. Again, this is similar to Qabalistic practices in which the magician moves up, down, or following the paths of serpents or lightning bolts, between and through the sephira. Following these practices, narratives and diverse ideas may come to you as a result of conscious efforts to derive them or they can subtly replace the background presuppositions of your life and generate almost-unnoticed shifts in attitude and awareness.

Once again, these techniques are general guidelines for practices that might continue for years—or a lifetime. Hopefully, as you get involved in mining relevant stories from your mind, specific details will emerge with greater clarity and frequency. And, again, these can be very simple, linear narratives, or they can be complex, non-linear, and featuring a cast of thousands. All the details are right there in your cloud of consciousness, your map of the world; you have all the tools and concepts you need to create your own kick-ass, sparkling, shining, mighty, mythic tales of woohoo.

eleven

Permanent Woohoo

Imprints

How would you like to have all the woohoo you could ever want, whenever you'd like, forever? Permanent, or nearly permanent, neurological change is possible—it happens every day. The usual rules apply: intensity, duration, and novelty change the way the brain organizes itself, both physiologically and psychologically. If an experience is really, really intense, lasts a really long time, and is totally, mind-blowingly new to us, the change can be dramatic. And if the new information carried by the experience encourages fundamental change in the way we think and behave, then the changes may be global, influencing every part of the brain.

In classic animal behavior studies, Konrad Lorenz proposed a type of learning that appeared to be a part of the basic biological drives of birds and mammals. He noticed that at certain points in an animal's life, it seems to be more susceptible to very suddenly taking on various preferences and life directives. For instance, he found that when a baby bird hatched from its egg, it would bond with the first thing that it saw. Usually, in a natural setting, that would be mommy bird, however, in laboratory settings Lorenz enticed birds to bond with ping-pong balls and other inanimate objects. When fully grown, these birds continued to identify with the ping-pong balls and would ultimately attempt to mate with them. It seemed that much of an animal's psyche would form around these deeply learned patterns, which Lorenz called *imprints.* That is, if a bird imprints on a ping-pong ball, it identifies with that ball to the point where it believes and bases its behavior on the knowledge that it is, in fact, a ping-pong ball. The bird would then choose to hang out with ping-pong balls and eventually chooses one for a mate.[1] In human terms, the acquisition of imprints would mark our rites of passage: birth, taking our place in the family, gaining communication skills, sexual maturation, marriage, menopause, death.

Timothy Leary proposed that imprints are acquired at biologically key moments in a human's life, that we form basic orientations for comfort, territoriality, language, and sex as we mature. He also proposed the possibility of "higher" imprints, which would account for basic orientations involved in such metaphysical concepts as somatic energy, synchronicity, meta-programming, and cosmic consciousness. Taking it beyond Lorenz, Leary believed that imprints could be acquired not only at the biologically preordained moments, but at moments of extreme stress, shock, ecstasy, and so on. More specifically, he proposed that chemical agents such as LSD could induce states in the human brain that would allow for re-imprinting or new imprints to be formed.[2]

In this paradigm, most of the learning we do falls into the category of *conditioning*. Learning that your friend's telephone number has changed, or which bus to take to get to work would be considered conditioning—and if you don't reinforce this kind of knowledge or behavior, you could conceivably forget it. Imprinting is a much more intense and permanent kind of learning that sets our basic self-concepts, our sexual preferences, our basic personality traits, our meta-programs, and our general strategies for learning and approaching the world. This relates more to the structure of what we learn and creates patterns for how we deal with the content.

Lorenz's theories were created before neuroscientists began to suspect the processes of neuroplasticity. Based on what we know now, there seems to be no clearly delineated boundary between conditioning and imprinting, but more of a gradient between the two. For our purposes, when, through intensity, novelty, or duration, neuroplasticity reaches a point where changes are made globally in the brain, we'll call that imprinting.

Initiation

Magicians and shamans have long taken advantage of these tendencies in the human brain. Imprinting is important to the concept of *initiation*. Initiation in a shamanistic or magical tradition is usually marked by a ritual that either celebrates a major neurological change in the candidate, or induces major neurological change in the candidate. The first type is more common in contemporary magical societies, but nonetheless, the emphasis is on acknowledging a change in personal epistemology on a deep, "hard-wired" level—an imprint, in Lorenz-speak. The second form of initiation is more common in indigenous shamanistic settings in which the initiation ritual induces intense neuroplasticity (an imprint, again) by use of shock, fear, pain, fasting, exhaustion, ecstasy, altered states, etc. When the point of imprint vulnerability (intense neuroplasticity) is reached, the new epistemology, the new personal narrative, is installed through ritual. The candidate leaves behind his or her old life and becomes a full member of the tribe or a shaman. (Of course, the contemporary magical initiations may also induce change and the traditional shamanistic ones also may celebrate turning points in the candidate's life, as well as inducing neurological change.) In some magical and shamanistic traditions, the point of susceptibility may be induced by the use of psychoactive drugs. While this remains fairly controversial in our society, what we know about the gene expression of the psychedelic experience makes a very plausible case for Leary's ideas about LSD and imprinting.[3] This may suggest both the possibilities of the use of entheogens and also their dangers; consciously or ritually oriented use can be enormously useful while random or recreational use may open us up to unwanted imprints that can be very difficult to change back.

Which brings us to a major point about initiation: these are deep and, for practical purposes, permanent changes that can affect many, if not all, aspects of life. Be very, very sure that it is what you want before inducing deep neurological change. Most changes that we choose to make in our lives and most issues that we decide to address can be effectively completed and resolved with much simpler methods. Usually we choose to work within our existing imprints, within the narrative landscape already familiar to us, rather than, in effect, changing our whole world.

Rites and Wrongs

In terms of what we have discussed so far, initiation is a way to make major rewrites to the personal narrative that defines the sense of self. These narratives can be mundane in nature or mythic in scope. Some of the initiation-like rite of passage rituals that we find, naturally occurring so to speak, in our society tend to reinforce the cultural status quo of standardized narratives. A child's first day at school is often a scary one, yet the child knows that this is a part of growing up and becoming an adult human. The fear can be enough to induce extreme neuroplasticity, yet the lessons imprinted are rarely those about reading, writing, or arithmetic; they are about the child's place among his or her peers, about the hierarchy and authority of the teachers, and societal roles in general.

Likewise, marriage rituals can induce neuroplasticity via fear, pomp and spectacle, exhaustion, group participation, and the liberal use of intoxicants. While these can be beautiful rituals and absolutely wonderful if consciously chosen and directed, in their usual form they reinforce standard societal concepts of family and sexual relationships whether they are appropriate for those involved or not. Indeed, marriage rituals often seem more effective at imprinting gender roles than the stated intent of bonding-for-life. In some contemporary cultural settings, the unspoken presupposition of the wedding ritual is that only when you are married do you take your place as a full, adult member of the group. The current controversy over gay marriage probably reflects more about the nature of marriage as a culturally sanctioned imprinting ritual than some of the political and religious ideas commonly expressed during debate.

If we accept only the narratives our society hands to us, our lives will follow the script of an old TV sitcom. Life rarely follows such simplistic narratives, and things can get pretty confusing if our brain is following a predictable *Father Knows Best* plot while the world offers up the complexity and diversity of real life. Use these techniques to give the story of your life some woohoo.

Initiation rituals can be used to improve your life or hinder it. In many parts of the world, a common shamanistic and magical initiation rite involves the simulated or near death of the candidate. In Inuit shamanism, for instance, the initiate is buried in snow, as if dead, and left until nearly so. Upon his or her exhumation and resurrection, the subject is given the symbols and knowledge of the tribal shaman, which, following such a ritual, will be etched deeply upon the brain.[4] In Haitian voodoo, however, a similar ritual is used to create the legendary zombies. The subject is given a drug made from a fish neurotoxin that simulates death, is buried, and then later exhumed. Upon "revivification," the subject is told that he or she is, in fact, dead and has been resurrected at the pleasure of the sorcerer. The subjects take on an imprint in which they believe they are willing "undead" servants.[5]

Okay, so that's the caveat before you get involved in the massive rewiring of your neurology—make sure any changes are something that improves your life, something you have chosen and can appreciate. Drone or free individual, zombie or shaman, it's up to you.

The other warning of note here is that with many of the traditional methods, you could hurt yourself or go just that little bit beyond "near death" into the real thing. In fact, that's the point. Without the possibility of real danger, the candidate's commitment to the ritual may be incomplete and the intensity insufficient. With some knowledge of the factors that contribute to neurological change, however, initiation rites can be created that are not only much safer, but full of woohoo as well. Fear can build intensity, but so can ecstasy.

Permanent Structures

The actual rituals employed in initiation are similar to the ritual structures used in other contexts. The difference comes from the increased intensity, duration, or novelty. Intensity may be the most common factor in these methods, though we do also find duration and novelty. For instance, duration may be applied in techniques that employ fasting or isolation, such as a "vision quest," in which the candidate is sent out into the wilderness to wait for a particular experience. In this kind of ritual, the candidate is given operative metaphors and mythology prior to leaving on the quest—the tales of ancestors or gods who have an interest in him or her, for instance—and when the intensity and duration of the experience reach a threshold level, the vision is obtained and the candidate's life is changed. The mythic narrative may be supported by prayer, chanting, dancing, drumming, or dreaming techniques throughout the quest.

Often the rituals are quicker and more intense. In some cultures, rites of passage are marked by ritual circumcision, scarring, or tattooing and the pain from these activities drives neurological change that helps to define the candidate's place in the society. Similar techniques can be used for more personal initiation rites. Some people will get tattoos or piercings that represent symbolic change in personal narrative or a dedication to a particular path. If this is performed in ritual circumstances, it can be quite effective and, indeed, permanent.

Sex rites can be quite powerful. Arousal and infatuation may cause neuroplasticity related to interpersonal bonding. Orgasm, particularly ones experienced as being fully satisfying, can induce change in the brain. Sexual activities that push one into novelty, or induce intense emotional states through the breaking of cultural taboo may also be quite powerful agents of neuroplasticity.

Dancing, running, walking, martial arts, and other kinds of physical movement can be powerful stimuli for neuroplasticity. For the most part, these must be of considerable intensity, duration, or novelty. However, movement has such a strong correlation with neuroplasticity,[6] incorporating even small amounts of movement can benefit most ritual techniques.

Other activities that, when pushed to extreme woohoo, may also be of use include chanting, singing, spinning, pranayama, firewalking, bungee-jumping, skydiving, high diving, spacewalking, childbirth, stage fright, blood loss, asphyxiation, fasting, and pretty much anything else that takes you to the extremes of human experience. Some of these are really dangerous, and the danger is part of their effectiveness. Again, this kind of initiation ritual is to be used only with great forethought—and the safer methods are usually just as effective. Ecstasy will change your brain as well as fear.

The following exercise introduces more intense neuroplasticity-inducing experiences to the ritual frames we have already explored.

Exercise 11.1 Initiation Ritual Frame

- **Select a set of elements and develop a cloud** as in the "Elementary Cloud" and "Silver Lining" techniques. Include as much detail as possible. Explore every combination of drawing in, stepping into, and evoking and invoking at every stage of the process.
- **Make great big entities for each of your elements** and place them in appropriate places. Have actual humans step into them and perform in their roles, if possible.
- **Internalize and externalize the symbols of your elements** and the overall shape of your cloud as much as possible. This may include developing rhythms or chants for each element, creating visual symbols to place within view, verbal descriptions or poetry, and anything else you can think of to place the symbols before your senses and in your mind. If you have humans performing in the roles of the god/esses, they can chant, drum, sing, draw, or engage in other activities specific to the entities.

- Move through this internal and/or external environment as you **use a technique to induce extreme neuroplasticity.** Enflame yourself with praying, dance your ass off, expand the hell out of your mind, take yourself well beyond your previous experience.
- **Maintain continuous exposure** to the metaphor/elements/entities that define the desired imprint before, during, and immediately after any neuroplasticity-inducing activities.
- When the ritual is complete, **reabsorb all imaginings and go enjoy your life.**

Once again, these general guidelines can be adapted to a wide variety of methods and for diverse content. It's your mind; make the ritual your own.

twelve

The Group Mind

The Third Mind

In their collaborative collection of essays and stories, *The Third Mind,* William Burroughs and Brion Gysin offered the idea that "When you put two minds together, there is always a third mind, a third and superior mind, as an unseen collaborator."[1] It also may stand to reason that when we put more than two minds together, a similar process gives us a group mind. Like singular human minds, group minds may be conflicted and discordant to varying degrees, or they may be coherent and single of purpose. The group mind functions as a collection of entities much the way we can consider one mind to have component entities. If the human entities are misaligned or have divergent purposes, the group mind will reflect that. If the component humans fit well together and can reach agreement or consensus, the group mind can become a more successful collaborator.

On the neurological level, our mirror neurons and theory of mind functions tend to blur the boundaries between individuals. Information flows between us consciously through language and media and unconsciously through facial expressions and other ideomotor indicators that our mirror neurons and modeling faculties read and respond to.

Mirror neurons respond strongly to those who move, dress, speak, and behave like we do. When we join in with others who look, sound, and act similarly, we feel as if we have become part of something. We have all experienced common phenomena that demonstrate this principle. In a classroom or testing environment, where everyone is sitting the same way, looking at, listening to, and doing the same things, we tend to fall in synch with each other. If one student coughs, the cough migrates around the room. If one person shifts in his or her seat or rustles papers, the seat-shifting and paper-rustling proves contagious. Similarly, a yawn may make the rounds of a group of friends, as may laughter, a gesture, an itch, a phrase, or an idea—all demonstrating our interconnectedness through neurology. Even better, when we sing, chant, or play music together; when we dance together; or when we make love, our common, mirroring behaviors blur the boundaries between one person and another. In such states of deep rapport, we mutually follow each other's lead, and the resulting behavior is not born of any one person.

In a more nefarious form, when large groups of people are directed to all do the same things—as when a military leader demands that troops dress, march, and behave the same way, or when a cult leader encourages his flock to drink the Kool-Aid—patterns of thought and beliefs may also spread quickly. This concept is frequently used by political forces to sway public opinion or to influence elections. When George W. Bush ran for presidential election and re-election in the United States, his campaign rallies were carefully controlled and were packed with enthusiastic supporters, many purportedly bused in from more distant locations, to give the impression of mass approval.[2] When Barack Obama ran for president in 2008, canvassers were instructed to tell undecided voters that many of their neighbors and peers were voting for Obama, which helped to develop a very successful "me too" effect.[3] Wilhelm Reich suggested that being a part of mass movements gives us a mystical sense of being part of something larger than ourselves.[4]

For the most part, however, the group minds we encounter each day are benign, if not beneficial. We identify these as our family, friends, clubs, organizations, movements, schools, and religions, and being a part of these group minds is a normal and healthy part of being human. It is how our neurology is wired. We have evolved as social organisms that devote a great deal of brainpower to mirroring and modeling each other. Everyone around you is also inside you, and you are inside them.

Memetic Entities

And of course the clever modeling centers in our brains can find entities in patterns of information that involve groups of people. We relate to institutions such as governments and churches as if they were big, if somewhat confusing, parents, family members, or friends. Government is "big brother" and the church is "the body of Christ."

> *Schools of thought, political ideologies, religious beliefs, corporate structures, forms of government—and much else—depend on the attention of humans to exist and they have built-in abilities to perpetuate, to include more humans, and even to reproduce. These self-perpetuating thought-forms, for our purposes here, are called "memetic entities." "Democracy" is a memetic entity, as is "Aikido," "Cognitive Behavioral Therapy," "Jazz," "Buddha," "Beelzebub," "Sherlock Holmes," "the English Language," and Atem. They are patterns of information that act with autonomy across time and yet interact with humans on many levels. All of the given examples became manifest through the interaction of human minds, some obviously by an individual, others less obviously by changes in culture.*[5]

Working in Groups

Think about it this way: the continual flow of information between all of us on an unconscious level, through ideomotor response and our mirror neuron systems suggests that, as religions and philosophies have proclaimed for eons, we are all one. That little area in the right frontoparietal lobe that tells each one of us, "I am me," creates an illusion of separateness, but mostly we are always connected to others. Within that single great human entity, that functions on a level that we, as individuals, have difficulty perceiving, are smaller pockets of interaction. These are the group minds and memetic entities. Humans appear to be wired this way and we also use that same wiring to perform some of our magical tasks.

So it can be really, really helpful to work your magick in the company—and with the participation—of others. Any entity beyond the strictly personal is living in the neurology-mediated information flow, the *noosphere*. This includes the commonly known gods and goddesses, angels, demons, fictional characters, and all other memetic entities. Even if you are all alone in your secret magical temple, if you work with an entity found in grimoires or religious texts, you are interacting with the minds of everyone else who has contributed, over time, to these entities. How much better, then, to physically join with others in group invocation, to fully activate and employ your mirror neuron system? We're talking about major woohoo.

The more popular memetic entities have their own congregations and places of worship, including churches, mosques, synagogues, cinemas, theme parks, concert halls, office buildings, and factories. It's easy enough to find people who want to participate in the rites of Jesus, Mickey Mouse, or the Grateful Dead. Where do we find co-experimenters to explore our lesser-known, newly found, or newly created entities? Sometimes the answers lie right in front of us. We participate in group minds every day, including family, friends, classes, coworkers, and the other impatient people in line at the post office. The following exercise has been used by a wide variety of different groups as a means to explore group minds and to develop rapport within the group. That's not limited to magical orders, moots, or meetups—almost any group of people that works or plays together can benefit from these processes, although perhaps not the impatient people at the post office. (Hint: You don't always have to explain that what you're doing is magick. Sometimes it's easy enough just to say it's fun, or will help us get to know each other, or that it might illustrate an interesting principle of neuroscience.) There are also Meta-Magick practice groups in various parts of the world—check meta-magick.com/groups.html for current listings and contact information. If you don't think you have others to work with yet, read through the steps of the exercise and imagine what kinds of opportunities you may have in the future to practice this way.

Exercise 12.1 Group Mind Ritual

- **Each group member develops his or her own Energy Flow Gesture** based on a particularly pleasant and empowering experience. While breathing deeply and evenly, each person brings his or her flow to a strong, powerful level. When that level has been reached, each will let the feeling of the flow find expression as a movement or gesture. Ask yourself, "If this feeling were a movement, what would it be?"
- **Working in pairs, each takes time to learn the other person's movement or gesture.** Partners will demonstrate their movements for each other as often as is necessary to learn them. Use as little verbal cueing as possible. Do it silently if you can.
- Then, facing each other, **each will return to his or her own movement**, repeating it over and over, while keeping eyes open and observing the other partner.
- As each group member watches his or her partner, they begin to incorporate elements of his or her movement into their own. **Each pair**

develops a "partner movement," a compromise or aggregate movement that both practice identically.

- **Partners practice the "partner movement" together** for another minute.
- Each partner pair will meet with another partner pair. **Each pair will teach their partner movement to the other pair,** so that both pairs can do both movements.
- Partners will then revert to their own partner movement, repeating it while observing the other partner pair, who will be repeating their own partner movement. Gradually, **each pair will integrate elements from the other pair's partner movement until a "foursome movement" is developed.**
- **Continue to practice the foursome movement together** for at least another minute.
- The entire group will then convene and **foursomes will each demonstrate their movements,** so that everyone can perform all the foursome movements.
- Foursomes will then revert to their own foursome movement, repeating it while observing the other foursomes. Gradually, **each person will integrate elements from the other foursomes until a "group movement" is developed** together (or if this proves difficult, until they are showing signs of deeper rapport, including laughter, smiling, and synchronous unconscious movements).

- **The group forms a circle, each participant facing the center, and practices the group movement** (or however close they have come to one) for at least another minute.
- **Everyone stops where they are and takes notice of how they feel** at that moment.
- **Each person develops their own energy flow for the feeling** they have at that particular moment.
- **Each person externalizes his or her own energy flow and places it in the same place in the center** of the circle.
- **Group members breathe into the combined energy flows.**
- Communicating silently with thoughts or with ideomotor testing, **each participant can communicate with the entity** as the rest of the ritual proceeds. Possible questions to ask the entity include: *What do I call you? What can you teach me? How can I be more aware of information on the level of the group? How can I facilitate increased rapport or consensus with others in my life?*
- One at a time, going around the circle, **each participant steps into the center**, stepping into the entity for a minute or so, noting any changes in state, then returning to the circumference.
- When all group members have had a turn stepping in, **each person then reabsorbs just as much energy as he or she originally put in and the ritual is brought to a close.**

- Participants take a few minutes to **discuss the experience.**

Just as individual consciousnesses have energy flows that are rich with submodality information, group minds can also develop their own metaphoric energy. The Group Vortex Ritual is a great way to encourage interaction and to build up group energy for a unified purpose.

Exercise 12.2 Group Vortex Ritual

- **Participants stand in a circle,** facing the center.
- A quality to invoke is agreed upon and **each group member creates their own energy flow** for that quality.
- **A direction, clockwise or counterclockwise, is decided upon.**
- At a given signal, **each person sends/imagines their energy flow flowing in the decided direction to the person next to them.** This continues for at least a few minutes as a continuous cycle of energy is developed.
- At a given signal, **everyone takes one step backward** out of the cycling energy flow, leaving the cycling vortex within the cycle.
- **Participants breathe deeply and exhale into the cycling vortex.**
- The group takes some time for everyone to **communicate with the vortex entity**, in whatever way each finds best.

- In addition to whatever other personal questions each person might have, they **ask the entity what part of their body could use some of the vortex energy.**
- **Each participant diverts some of the vortex energy and directs it toward whatever part of their body the entity suggested.**
- Each participant, in turn, may **stand inside the vortex for a minute or two** and observe any differences in state they may experience.
- **Everyone takes a step forward,** back to their original positions in the vortex.
- **Everyone then reabsorbs just as much energy as they originally put in and the ritual is brought to a close.**
- Participants take a few minutes to **discuss the experience.**

Decision Processes

Sometimes the thought processes of group minds can be complex and difficult to follow. Other times, however, decision-making processes may be adopted in a more conscious fashion. These are usually pretty obvious and consist of contracts, bylaws, constitutions, and other such documents that outline the behavior and protocol of individuals in relation to larger entities, various subgroups within entities, and the group minds in relation to the world. Such documents are numerous and, in their sum total, constitute the rules and infrastructure of the really big entity that we call our society.

To keep it simple, we'll focus on three types of decision-making processes that can apply to the kinds of groups that may work with these exercises. There are times when each of these will be appropriate, there are also situations in which they may be blended together to some extent, and participants are encouraged to experiment with variation.

1. **The decision-maker:** One person makes decisions for the entire group.
2. **Majority rules:** Decisions are voted upon by the group and those with the most votes are used.
3. **Consensus:** Each participant has input and the decision is adjusted, added to, subtracted from, and modified until all concerns are addressed.[6]

Each of these different decision-making processes will influence the nature of a group mind at least as much as any other factor. Which decision process will offer more woohoo will depend on the particular members and goals of the group.

Syncretism

Playing with decision processes can provide a quicker method (usually) for observing how our gods and goddesses came to be than waiting many years to observe syncretism in action. Syncretism is the process whereby various different opinions, beliefs, and concepts are combined to produce a unified religion or entity. Some examples of syncretism may be familiar to some readers, including the adoption of indigenous pagan holidays and symbols in the practices of Christianity as it spread throughout the world: trees, mistletoe, and other symbols of solstice celebration combined with the story of Jesus to produce the modern celebration of Christmas; or pre-Christian fertility symbols, eggs, bunnies, and even the name Easter (from the same roots as Eostre, Astarte, and Ishtar: female fertility goddesses) combined with New Testament lore, to create the holiday of egg hunts and the baby Jesus. Figure that each time some new element was added to the invocation ritual that we call "holiday celebration," some decision process was also invoked. A pope or cleric or scholar proclaimed the symbolism, perhaps; or a body of priests, bishops, or wise men took a vote; or bits and pieces were added or subtracted as each group or individual provided input.

Syncretism gets even more interesting and fun on the level of entities, and the long history of meeting and merging memetic entities has given us more animal-headed or animal-bodied entities than can be counted: gods and demons with unusual numbers of arms, legs, breasts, and other body parts—with blue skin, green skin, purple skin, and every other variation that can be imagined. If we think of these diverse critters as memetic entities, with each meme analogous to a gene, syncretism represents the reproduction and evolution of our imaginary friends.

Practice groups—or you and your friends on a Saturday night—can explore the process of syncretism in a relatively quick (compared to the centuries usually involved) and fun way. Group Meta-Deities can be very intense, very serious, or very, very silly, depending on your goals and purposes. Play around with different kinds of decision processes and notice how your entities take different forms and offer different kinds of information. Notice which methods build the most woohoo into your entity and into your life.

Exercise 12.3 Group Meta-Deity

- **Participants sit in a circle and a banishing is performed** to clear the space. This can be as simple as each participant practicing Expansion/Contraction breathing, filling and clearing the work area.
- **The group selects an objective or quality** for which they would like to create a group-mind deity.
- **The elements of that objective or quality are identified.** In a small group, each participant can suggest one element. In a larger group, a fixed number can be agreed upon and suggestions can be ratified by consensus, vote, or decision-maker.
- **Each participant imagines a humanoid figure** in the center of the circle and makes appropriate adjustments to the figure as the ritual proceeds.
- **Each participant, in turn, makes a suggestion concerning the physical attributes of the entity.** These may concern the sex of the entity, its size, color, shape, posture, gesture, facial features, number of limbs, special effects and features, and so on. Almost anything is fair game as long as it represents, in the mind of the suggesting participant, that objective, overall quality, or any of the elements. For instance, in seminars we have developed godforms with

six arms, green skin, gills, sharp teeth, feline bodies, etc.

- **Participants simultaneously develop state entities for each of the chosen elements and place these into the group entity.** For instance, if the elements are speed, intelligence, and patience, then all participants will develop their own "speed" state entity and place it into the godform, all will develop their own for intelligence and add them to the mix, and all will develop state entities for patience and place them into the godform.
- **Participants breathe into the godform** and continue to offer the godform breath and attention through the remainder of the ritual.
- **Each participant, in their own mind, asks the godform for one syllable of the god/dess's name.** When each has added their syllable, the sounds are combined to create the full name of the god/dess.
- **Each participant then asks the god/dess what offering or ritual would be appropriate to add more attention and energy to the god/dess.** If these are practicable, then they are performed.
- **Each participant then asks the god/dess for any information it might be able to offer specific to their own situation.**
- One at a time, **participants step into the godform,** and experience the state for a minute or two.

- The group then decides if the god/dess is to be given a place to inhabit, or if it is to be reabsorbed by the participants. **The god/dess is then either given leave to inhabit its new domain or is absorbed.**
- **The space is then banished** again.
- **Participants reflect on their experience** and record any relevant information.

Each time we've worked with a Meta-Deity has been a unique experience. Descriptions of any one of them might not give you the woohoo of your own group creation, but might demonstrate how diverse elements from each participant can join to create a unified entity. In a 2007 workshop in Seattle, for instance, our group created an entity dedicated to Magick itself, a true Meta-Magick entity. The entity's name turned out to be SLA-OO-DAM-SCI-BA-SSS, and its elements were motivation, perseverance, efficacy, imagination, sensitivity, and wisdom. SLA was human-sized, hermaphroditic, and had a forked tongue, monkey tail, blue skin, six arms, piercing green eyes, and wings. The offerings that the entity wanted were words, chanting, transmuted gold, stroking, prayers, and communication. With our permission, SLA went on to inhabit a local park. Each one of us gained some personal insight into our magical practice from the interaction with SLA. The entity has also demonstrated a little bit of memetic survival instinct, too, by wanting to be included in this book.

The Celebration of Woohoo

Most of us are probably familiar with forms of invocation that involve celebrations within a group. These include various festivals of the seasons and other holidays, solemn ceremonies, and joyous parties. Very often the actions of invocation involve the environment itself, the building or space that holds the festival, and everything that participants bring into the space. The following ritual uses decision-making processes and group invocation techniques to really increase intensity, duration, and novelty of an invocation. It can be adapted for groups of any size but, up to a point, provides the most woohoo with larger numbers of participants.

Exercise 12.4 Group Environmental Ritual

- Either by single-person decision, majority vote, or consensus, **the group decides on an overall quality and component elements to invoke.**
- **Each element is assigned to a physical location** in the ritual area. This arrangement may be based in group agreement or may fit the necessities of the space.
- For each zone, **participants are assigned actions**, including but not limited to creating a visual symbol, a rhythm, a melody, words, a dance or gesture, an offering or ritual act. For instance, if the elements of the ritual are Wisdom, Patience, and Adaptability, one person would be assigned to create a visual symbol for Wisdom, one would create a rhythm for Wisdom, one would create a visual symbol

for Patience, one would create the rhythm for Patience, etc. If there are fewer people, actions can be combined in a variety of ways. For instance, one person could be assigned to create all of the actions for one element. (Pat creates symbol, rhythm, etc., for Wisdom.) Alternatively, one person could create visual symbols for each and every element, someone else could create rhythms for each element, and so on. Another way to adapt for a smaller group or shorter amount of time would be to limit the actions in each zone, perhaps to just a symbol and words, or whichever tasks the group or leader agrees on.

- To accomplish each task, each can use one of the following methods:
  - Create an internal energy flow and allow the words, rhythm, movement, symbol, or act to arise from the intensified feeling of the flow.
  - **Create a state entity for the element and get assistance from the entity** in creating the symbol, rhythm, melody, etc.
  - Create a full god/dess and step into it, allowing the words, rhythm, etc., to arise from the intensified feeling of the invocation.
- When each ritual element has been developed in this way, **the entire group convenes and, beginning with one element, everybody performs each action as a group.** That is, everyone looks at the symbol together (or draws it in the air), plays the rhythm together, says the

words together, and so on until the full group has performed every action in every zone.

- **Participants may then wander about in the space**, visiting the different elemental zones individually. When entering a zone, a participant joins in with whatever actions are already taking place in the zone or begins one, continuing with activities specific to that zone until he or she leaves for another zone.
- At a prearranged time or signal, **the group convenes as a whole in the center of the space.** Each continues performing the action that he or she was performing at the time to convene.
- **Participants make their best effort to unify the actions into a harmonious, aesthetic composition.**
- When the actions have blended and been performed that way for a time, **everyone stops and remains silent for a while**, taking notice of what perceptions and states they are presently experiencing.
- **The ritual is brought to a close with a single action performed by all**, perhaps created as an amalgam or sample of the blended actions from the previous steps.
- **Participants withdraw from the ritual area and discuss their experience.**

✧✧✧

thirteen

Speculation

Is That All?

So, at this point, we have a model of magick that suggests that invocation is based in the natural tendency of the human brain to create, within itself and without, functioning minds—entities. When thinking about a god or goddess, we use the same systems and functions in the brain as we use for social interaction, processing of metaphor, and self concept. The mirror neurons, default network, and the self-concept areas in the right parietal lobe help to build our internal experiences when we daydream or dream about others and when we define the boundaries of that unique entity sometimes referred to as "myself." The basic action of invocation involves the mapping of entities with submodalities that signify godhood onto the model that we have for "self." Instant magick—just add woohoo.

When we theorize that our "spiritual" experiences have some basis in neurology, it may be tempting to decide that such experiences are purely a product of brain chemistry and have no further significance. That may well be the case, if we eventually learn that the electro-chemical reactions of our nervous system represent the most fundamental level of existence. But we already know that they do not. The theories we have explored here, a tiny fraction of what we know about human neurology, are ultimately metaphors that we use to explain the complexity of the clouds of probability that physicists assert compose the atoms and molecules of our brains, just as they do all matter. At some point in the near future, when our understanding of the world further evolves, we may think these theories as crude and primitive as earlier explanations of the luminiferous ether or the geocentric universe. For now, our neuroscientific model can be useful; if we base our practices upon it, we can achieve results that align with our goals and predictions. And while we experiment in this way, let's bear in mind that what happens in the brain may be only a small fraction of the overall explanation for spiritual, magical, or woohooful experiences.

Unexplained Phenomena

Even just on the neurobiological level, the implications may be as miraculous as anything occult science has ever suggested. There are a few really wonderful phenomena that Meta-Magick practitioners regularly report. We'll call the first one Deep Synchronicity. The most common form of this is when a practitioner "creates" an entity from his or her own personal feelings, memories, and experiences—and then later discovers that the name and attributes of the entity are exactly the same as an obscure (or not so obscure) god or demon from ancient mythology. Simple evocations have yielded traditional Goetic demons for practitioners who professed no previous knowledge of the Keys of Solomon. In one case, a practitioner who was seeking advice about what kind of business he could start called up a goddess who claimed her name was Atuma. She stood by a pool of water and showed the practitioner a sign made by touching her thumbs and forefingers together in a downward-pointing triangle. When he told me about it, I recognized the gesture as an Egyptian symbol for water, but the practitioner had no idea about this. We both googled the goddess's name and learned that Atuma was the name of a city in the ancient Middle East that was sacred to a goddess of the same name. The importance of the city was in the pools of water found in an otherwise arid region. The practitioner's business, by the way, turned out to concern beverages.

That's the next phenomenon: the usefulness of information. If you've come this far into the book and practiced the exercises, hopefully you have learned some useful things not only about the form of your woohoo, but also about the content of your hopes, dreams, aspirations, and goals. Whenever we contact entities in group situations—and reports from solo practitioners also frequently support this—individuals often learn specific information that helps them to achieve their desires: what to do, who to talk to, what to ask, which ritual acts to perform, and so on.

Then we get the weirder levels of synchronicity. Some of these can be very specific. For instance, ritual participants may see visions of other places, then, either immediately or in the very near future, find themselves in exactly those places. Or we may think of specific objects, only to find them or receive them after the ritual. Some of this may be simple wish fulfillment, but sometimes these occurrences seem particularly improbable. I once worked with a young woman who wanted to overcome a fear of flying so that she could take a trip that she had planned. I had her take the feeling of her fear, evoke it as a state entity, and transform it into a positive entity. As the positive entity, it turned bright green, red, and white. When she got on the airplane soon after, she was pleasantly surprised to find that the entire inside of the plane was decorated in green, red, and white. She had a wonderful trip.

With synchronicity, it's often best to refrain from attributing cause and effect to your ritual work and just to appreciate how events may resonate with each other. The Group Meta-Deity mentioned in Chapter 12, SLA-OO-DAM-SCI-BA-SSS, as I said, was left to inhabit a local park. Shortly after our ritual, odd things started happening in the park. Among other occurrences at the park, there were unexplained smells and tar began to bubble up from the ground. These were demonstrated to be harmless, but nonetheless encouraged a general cleanup of the park grounds (and underground—they drilled into the ground to pump out the tar). One might say that hidden information about the park was revealed that enabled people to improve it. Was SLA-OO-DAM-SCI-BA-SSS responsible? Who can say? It was just interesting that the events began to occur within days of our entity taking up residence.

Sometimes the information is there but, at least to my mind, hard to interpret. Some years back, my wife and I purchased a property where we intended to renovate an old building to use as a studio. The building was set on many acres of dense forest. Just around that time, I went to a conference at which there was a workshop on psychometry, the art of psychically getting information from objects. I passed around the key to my new building without telling anyone what it was or anything about the property. The first person I handed it to concentrated on the key and then said, "The forest wants to be thinned out." His girlfriend, who was sitting next to him, assured me that he had weird psychic abilities when it came to trees. I thought it was cool that he knew we had a forest, but thought that cutting trees sounded destructive, and like too much work.

Later, when our building was ready, we gathered a small group of friends and had a group-mind ritual in which we created a group entity for prosperity. The prosperity entity told me, "Prosperity grows like a tree." I thought it was a nice metaphor. About a year later, I did a second ritual, by myself, sitting out in the woods in which I found the feeling of sitting there and evoked it as a state entity. The entity told me it would benefit me to thin the forest. Again, I thought it seemed like too much work for me with my single, underpowered chain saw. Finally, a couple years after that, I ran into a friend and we started talking about my land. He said, "Oh yes, I know that land. I once checked the logging records for that land and you have tens of thousands of dollars in standing timber." He gave me the phone number of a logging professional. In short, we did do some logging there, it helped us financially and, even better, the wildlife suddenly became more varied and numerous. The forest was thriving and happy. The rituals and the entities were working hard on this one, I was just a bit slow.

Shared experience across space, time, or the boundaries of self and other may occur. That is, an entity may give the same advice, experience, colors, sounds or feelings to two or more people independently. Participants in a group ritual may find themselves increasingly aware of what thoughts, experiences, and colors other participants are contributing.

Sometimes we observe odd phenomena related to time. For instance, a ritual may help us to understand something that happened in the past. Or we may become aware of branching probabilities and the outcomes that can result from each. Sometimes objects, ideas, beliefs, and even entire realities seem to jump from one probable timeline to another, or from very distant parts of one's timeline or cloud—from the distant past or the distant future, well beyond the span of the practitioner's life.

A Thought Experiment

So how do we explain this stuff? Again, I don't think we have any hard-and-fast theory that accounts for everything. Maybe it's all subjective, delusion and hallucination that results from messing around with our brains. On the other hand, maybe subjective delusion and hallucination are important ingredients in the fabric of the universe itself. It's all illusion, as Hindus believe. Or perhaps there's some middle ground.

How about a thought experiment? For this experiment let's stipulate that there is nothing in the universe except stuff—atoms, molecules, matter, and energy. Our brains are really just more stuff, atoms and molecules and so on. In this thought experiment, there is nothing that makes human matter any different than other matter. Just for now, imagine that there is no indwelling spirit, ghost in the machine or soul, except that which might exist in all matter; there is no external hand of a non-corporeal being pushing things around. It is all the same stuff—and it seems to have organized itself into "minds," if none other than the ones associated with the meat in our heads. The mind that you are using to think right now, based in the stuff crammed between your ears, is an amazingly complex device that recognizes patterns and divvies up what it perceives into me, you, him, them, cats, dogs, multinational corporations, nations, religions, gods, angels, demons, and other such entities. Do the entities exist as such until the human brain has recognized them as entities?

Maybe consciousness exists as a continuum and entities are its way of delineating itself. We recognize and delineate other entities, and they recognize and delineate us.

Some physicists suggest that our measurements determine what we ultimately perceive as the world. It is theorized that the spin or direction of a subatomic particle is indeterminate until a measurement is made. Not just that it is unknown; the particle doesn't have a set spin or direction until interaction with the physicist's consciousness makes it so. One school of physics argues that this kind of phenomenon only applies at the subatomic level. Others suggest that what happens on the subatomic level also applies to the macro level of stuff that we can normally perceive without special instruments. This is referred to in Meta-Magick as the concept of *making,* which we express with the metaphor, "A path is formed by walking on it."[1]

> *The final and possibly most crucial aspect of making is noticing what has been made. Measurement and testing bring the change or entity into sharply defined reality. You have to look back at the path to see that it has been formed.*[2]

Magical Epistemology

One interpretation of the physics of making is that at each point of measurement, the thing being measured is not just indeterminate, but actually exists in all possible states, in multiple universes. By measuring, our consciousness decides not only what state the particle or thing being measured will appear in, but which universe we navigate into. This has an interesting parallel with the concept of transderivational search. When transderivational search kicks in, the mind runs quickly through a range of possibilities. If the choices are of memories, then each memory is subject to reconsolidation, and submodalities or content may change as the mind runs through choices, or when we pull a single memory fully into consciousness. By the time it comes into conscious awareness, we've chosen a particular reality, a particular universe to inhabit in which the memory, as we now remember it, with whatever quality of woohoo it might have, is true.

If that's the case, then what we choose for the future on this unconscious level can equally become true. That is, our experiments with invocation may carry us into a universe in which we live lives of wonderful woohoo. Notice the emphasis on "unconscious." The process of transderivational search is guided by the default network, usually outside of our awareness. That's not to say that we can't influence the outcome of mental selection—you've already done it. By changing state through the process of invocation (or other means), we influence our brains to make selections that reflect that state. Remember? Sad people dwell on sad memories; happy people have happy memories. Anxious people make scary representations of their imagined future; fun people make their future even more fun.

A Zen koan asks, "Who is the master who makes the grass green?" We might also wonder about the master who tweaks our submodalities whenever we think.

We can influence the outcome of transderivational search in specific and fundamental ways. As our invoked entities increase in complexity toward full mind-states, they start to develop their own fundamental ways of perceiving and relating to the world. In the realm of human entities, we expect that it helps to think like an engineer to design a bridge, or like a politician to get elected, or like a mathematician if you want to understand advanced physics. Our imagined entities are similar in this regard; we expect that a magick entity will help us to understand or practice magick, that we'll be thinking of earthier things when we invoke an earth entity, or that Athena, goddess of wisdom (among other things), will help us to make wiser decisions. By creating entities who think or make decisions based on a specific set of presuppositions, we can use these highly detailed mind-states to change our own beliefs about the world. Step into Athena and let your default network choose differently and transport you into the world where wisdom is the highest criteria by which decisions are made. Athena's criterion may be expressed by the presupposition "All things can be guided by wisdom." In the mind-state world of a magick entity, we might find a higher-order rule of life to be expressed as "All things can be guided by magick."

Perhaps the presuppositions upon which we base our most fundamental beliefs can be altered—or we can transport ourselves into parallel worlds in which fundamental beliefs are very, very different. Some of the operating beliefs in our current universe (assuming you are in the same one in which I'm writing this!) include "matter is solid, liquid, or gas," "two objects cannot occupy the same space," "gravity pulls down," "Planet Earth is a big ball of stone with a molten nickel-iron core," "I am a human being and will be one until I die," and so on. How much of these presuppositions is real, external truth (if there is such a thing) and how much is encoded into our epistemology and linguistic structures at a very early age we cannot say for sure. These kinds of fundamental presuppositions cannot be changed by willpower, by wishing them to change, or by consciously trying to change them. If and when we do manage to change them through whatever means, the resulting beliefs may seem as utterly ordinary as the ones they replaced. On a conscious level, it might seem as if nothing has changed, or that we have realized something about the world that has always been that way. Then you get to write a book and convince others that the world has always been this way.

No matter how deeply we are able to change our epistemological basis for reality, the world that results must be at least somewhat internally consistent. That is, whatever the new presuppositions might be, they have to work according to the laws and tendencies of that world. A conscious belief that you can jump off a building and fly in a world where "gravity pulls down" is a basic presupposition—expressed in the very shapes and positions of everything and everyone around you—will probably end very badly. However, in that same world, if "gravity pulls down" can be part of the equation for a glide ratio or the lift necessary for a set of wings to overcome the downward pull, then flight may be possible, according to the laws of that world. Perhaps in the next universe over "levity pulls up" and scientists debate the possibility of manned descent.

Here's where that quality of wholeness comes into play once again. To be internally consistent, a world-map must be complete. Ultimately, everything in a world-map implies everything else, on some level, however obscure or infinitesimal that information might be. The moon that lights up our night sky pulls the oceans back and forth in easily observable tides. The tides influence the life cycles of sea organisms, which in turn affects global levels of oxygen, which has impact, small or large, on our general quality of life. All the other planets also exert their influence on the liquids, solids, and gases of Earth. These influences can be measured with instruments more sensitive than the human eye. Distant stars and galaxies also exert their forces, if only through their influence on the sun. It might take very sensitive telescopes and other instruments to measure the miniscule amount of influence that a distant star might have upon the Earth. Closer to home, the food you eat contributes to regional and global farming practices, availability and economics of agricultural resources, wages of farm and factory workers, the content of landfills, and so on. On the level of information, every person we see or think about plays upon our mirror neurons in ways that influence both state and physiology, however noticeably or minutely. Each of those people is similarly influenced by countless others, who in turn are affected by millions more. Every element of a congruent world-map implies and is in some way dependent upon every other element. The sum total constitutes a system and for a system to continue to function, it must exhibit wholeness.

So once again, here is that full-sensory story that we create inside our heads. Or are we inside of it? Being aware of our part in the intricacies of these worlds and minds within worlds and minds takes our speculation into the realm of mysticism. The pattern of wholeness is repeated again and again, in individual human minds and the mind-states and entities within each of us, in group minds, in the world-maps that individuals and groups create, and perhaps in the entire range of universes, the multiverse, that we shift through from moment to moment. This fractal reiteration is perhaps not so strangely reminiscent of the Hermetic axiom "As above, so below."

Self-Flex

Another interesting phenomena of this thought experiment occurs after we have explored a variety of mind states of different sizes and complexity. When we invoke and "think from" the perspective of a god/dess, a group mind, or a world-map, the part of the brain that tracks "self" starts to show a little more flexibility. This may be a natural function that helps us to be a useful part of our families, tribes, religions, businesses, and nationalities. For our purposes, it is possible to have experiences in which self becomes less important, or perhaps is extinguished entirely, at least for a little while. In contemporary mystical lore, these are called ego-death experiences, although we are probably talking about decreased activity in the right parietal lobe of the brain more than the death of that metaphoric entity of yore, the ego. These experiences give us a glimpse of our place in the greater systems of which we are a part. It is likely, for instance, that increased incidences of such selfless experiences in the 1960s, resulting from psychedelic drugs and spiritual practices, led directly or indirectly to the ecology movement and the peace movement.

The practice of invocation may sometimes (but not always!) rate lower on intensity and novelty than the ego-death of an acid trip, but over time the exploration of numerous entities, both large and small, creates an ability that might be described as "self-flex." This is the ability to identify with "selves" of more variety and scope and, at will, to suppress the "self" part of the brain to a greater or lesser degree. Traditional devotional practices were considered a path to samadhi, full identification of devotee and god. It may be that identification with a particular deity can decrease activity in that part of the right frontoparietal lobe as we experience the qualities, personality, and epistemology of the god/dess.

Until we can start scheduling Meta-Magicians for long-term brain scan studies, most of this remains speculation. However, if you read any of this and formed judgments or opinions about it, hopefully you did so based on the experiments you performed rather than the beliefs you previously held. If you found that you were making judgments about these ideas and have not yet practiced the exercises from the previous chapters, then please place those opinions on hold. Suspend judgment, go back and do the exercises, and then re-read this chapter.

fourteen

The Way of Woohoo

Your World is Your Medium

Some people treat the practice of magick as an end in itself, and there are systems of magick that support this idea. In the isolation of their inner sanctum, these practitioners delve into experiences of increasing complexity or intensity that hopefully lead to some ultimate knowledge or transformation. Who knows? Maybe they'll get there. The Way of Woohoo, however, is about being in the world, in your body, and living your life. We perform experiments and explore consciousness so that we will know how to take our insights and create excitement, intensity, wonder, mystery, and beauty all around us, so that we can re-create our world and life as an ongoing work of art.

Our neurology, as we understand it now, is built to support social interaction, communication, friendships, relationships, and participation in families, organizations, and group minds of every kind. Participation in our world usually means working, playing, hating, loving, talking to, entertaining, and generally sharing our experience with others. While solitude can be enjoyable and useful, it only remains that way for most people relative to the times when we actively join in the world of human and memetic entities. Our mirror neurons unconsciously share information about states, so use the techniques in this book to make a friend feel wonderful, to blow someone's mind, to turn a lover on mentally and physically, or to communicate your revelation about how the world has always been. It's simple: take yourself there first. Create wonderfully exquisite states for yourself and become an exemplar to others. Light the darkness, bring peace to the strife-torn, offer love to the lonely, and recognize the wholeness, uniqueness, and divine nature of every human you meet.

Your body is your instrument and your world is your medium. Really, it's all we have. So once again—how much do you want your own story to really rock? How exquisite, grand, powerful, intriguing, seductive, exciting, or mythic would you like your experience to be? What excites your neurons, strokes your sense of aesthetics, fulfills your philosophy, applies significance to your circumstance, or makes you scream and shout?

Invocation gives you the ability to draw qualities and skills into yourself, to think from different points of view and with the capabilities of different "minds" than the ones that you usually take for your own. Will you be fearless in the face of adversity? Strong when strength is required and comfortably flexible when it is time to yield? Will you become a great lover, a visionary artist, a world-changing scientist, a wonderful parent, a tireless athlete, an excellent student, a brilliant chess player, or the person who grows the biggest and tastiest tomatoes in the county? Whatever stories you create for your future, imagine them in whatever sensory detail you can, give them submodalities of amazing woohoo, and then leave them in your brain for your default network to process. As you think about your future, your default network can recall these imagined stories and details and reconsolidate them into the broader plot arc of your full-sensory creation, the story of your life.

The choices that you make will ultimately determine what kind of entity, inhabiting what kind of body, will be what others call your name and what you call "me." Will that entity be a random collection of states and selves and impulses, or can it align itself and become a cohesive, integrated being? That entity and all the component minds that constitute it make the choices that determine what kind of story we star in and what kind of world provides the setting for that tale. Our reality may be a consensus between the whole imaginary crowd of us, little and big, from embodied metaphors to gods and goddesses, all the other humans we perceive, and all the greater, multiple-human minds in which we participate.

Maybe you'll be able to bring woohoo into your life one decision at a time. Or maybe you'll be able to step boldly into that alternate universe where every moment of your life is an adventure of new woohoo. Either way, now is the time to imagine that woohoo-filled future that can be yours. So… how much woohoo can you do now?

Exercise 14.1 Future Pacing

- In what ways can you use what you have learned and experienced by practicing these exercises—in all areas of your life—in the coming days, weeks, months, and years?
- If *The Way of Woohoo* were to become more widely understood, what various effects might it have on individuals, groups, and society?
- What new techniques, rituals, or creative works do you think you can develop in your future, and what will be the ramifications of those?

appendix one

Sex

Something happened about 40,000 years ago that turned a pack of savannah-wandering apes into language-wielding, society-building humans. Fossil records show that our brains were already their present size about 250,000 years ago, but somehow we took our time figuring out how to activate the functions that produced cultural phenomena. Neuroscientist V. S. Ramachandran has hypothesized that the "great leap forward" in human society came in part as a result of activating the mirror neuron system in our protohuman ancestors. The mirror neurons enable imitative learning and also allow memes to spread very rapidly. Ramachandran suggests that it is possible that isolated tribes or individuals had, in fact, developed language, music, art, tools, and culture, but that, without a sophisticated, active mirror neuron system, the ideas quickly "dropped from the meme pool." Instead, once fortuitous circumstances brought about an innovation, the mirror neurons of the early humans—which had evolved for some other reason, perhaps—allowed the cultural tools and information to spread quickly.[1]

Ramachandran offers the idea that some of our vocalization ability, music, and, indeed, the rudiments of language, developed as part of our courtship rituals. A gestural language and vocalization allowed early humans to express and share emotions and to woo a mate. "Croonin' a toon," as Ramachandran says, rose in sophistication as our mirror neurons likewise developed. When one of our ancestors had an idea that went beyond the usual emotions or gonadic gratification, it had the opportunity to be transmitted quickly throughout the tribe and to neighboring tribes. Once we were able to express these ideas in real language, they spread even faster and had a snowball effect.

The development of mirror neurons began with sex, so that's as good a place as any to push the speculation. Let's say that these brain areas developed in part through natural selection. That is, they tended to aid the survival of the species. Apart from fleeing hungry carnivores, survival generally means reproducing, courtship, nesting, and providing the means to feed offspring. In short, these are the fundaments of a cultural code—all pretty much based in sex. The appearance of mirror neurons, for whatever reason, really made sex more complex, interesting, and raised it to eros—to the level of art. The human who could best express his or her emotions and urgency of rutting would get laid the most and pass on the linguistic, croonin', mirror neuron genes.

When the great leap forward jumped ahead, suddenly the neurology designed for effective courtship became something that we used to create metaphor and develop language skills. We used it to create religion, politics, and society. It appears that the fundaments of human communication, in almost every area of life, are based in our sex drive. Civilization itself may be one big courtship ritual. On a deep neurological level, it may well be that most things produced by humans were created as an attempt, directly or indirectly, to get laid. The Mona Lisa, the Great Pyramid of Giza, toasters, packing peanuts, computers, and, quite possibly, books. The Eiffel Tower, very likely. Religion and politics, no doubt. And all the entities that we can conceive of, invoke, or evoke are based in the neurology that we use for wooing a mate.

Indeed, entities seem to be a very direct part of the human courtship dance.

> *Almost every human on Planet Earth has another person living inside. That other person is our own Inner Babe. The Inner Babe is the projected complement of our identity and is just as real as God, Santa Claus, or the President of the United States. When we meet someone who demonstrates enough of the qualities of our Inner Babe, a cascade of neurochemical change begins, eventually leading to that confusing and blissful state of consciousness called "love." The Inner Babe is not exactly an ideal form in the sense that Joe might have had a thing for slim young women with dark hair. Or that he deeply appreciated a firm round ass packed into tight jeans. While these may have been factors in the arousal of*

> *Joe's undeniable lust, it must be noted that recognition of the Inner Babe is more often based on subtle behavioral cues: a tone of voice, a tilt of the head, a repeated pattern of eye movements, a way of breathing, a whiff of pheromone, or a certain rhythm of movement. The cues just start to add up and—wham! The immediate effects of the neurochemical cocktail include rapid heartbeat, changes in breathing, distortions in perception of time, feelings of euphoria, and full-on sexual arousal.... When two humans mistake each other for their Inner Babes and begin to bond through social rituals, the feedback loop can accelerate quickly. Many panic at this stage and some bail out. The intensity of sensation suddenly opens the mind to neurological change. Neurons find new directions for their signals. Perceptions become imprinted on the brain. A touch can linger forever, long after the physical contact is gone, a chance word can become a reason to exist.*[2]

The Inner Babe may be a close relative of other imaginary friends found in psychological lore, including the anima or animus, the female archetype found in the male mind and the male archetype found in the female. The Inner Babe is more personal. He or she is a sort of entity template that your mind creates from the anima/animus, processed through your mirror neurons to include behaviors, presuppositions, and ideomotor movements based on your own neurology. The Inner Babe is woohoo itself, the very form of an entity most likely to draw your attention, hold your fascination, and turn you on.

One common approach to sex magick involves partners imagining each other in the roles of gods or goddesses. The ritual becomes a metaphor for union with the deity, a form of invocation enhanced by the natural tendencies and drives of sex. That is, desire for your partner becomes ardor for your god or goddess. The physical involvement and intense feelings encourage neurological change that supports the invocation.

Sex obviously scores highly on the intensity scale. All the physiological factors contribute to intense states that can stimulate neuroplasticity in a big way. As the intensity and duration of arousal increase, even more woohooful states can be achieved that can be turned toward magical tasks. Orgasm itself induces a moment or three of sweeping neuroplasticity. Several forms of traditional sex magick are based on utilizing the process of arousal and orgasm.

> *If a man ardently wishes a force or power into being and guards this wish from the instant that he penetrates into the woman until the instant that he withdraws from her, his wish is necessarily fulfilled.—Paschal Beverly Randolph*[3]

If the wished-for "force or power" is an aspect of the man's (or woman's) own consciousness—a state, a desired quality, a change in behavior, and corresponding change in the world around him or her—then this may make neurological sense. If that same force or power is represented as a mind-state via the mirror neurons, then we have a means to imprint the complex, subtle, and lasting experiences of a god or goddess on our neurology. The following exercise provides a demonstration of one way to develop and maintain mind-states while dramatically building up intensity. Remember: the more woohoo, the better you will do!

Exercise A1.1 Sex God/desses

- Partners **banish the ritual space** using Expansion/Contraction breathing, the Lesser Banishing Ritual of the Entities, or a traditional method they may be familiar with.
- Cooperating together, partners use any of the methods previously described in this book to **create two godforms** (Instant God/dess, Instant Empowerment, Mastery Technique, or Group Meta-Deity). These can be chosen to be compatible with each other in whatever way the partners deem appropriate. For instance, if the partners are heterosexual, one entity can be male, the other female. If the entities are developed to the point where they have their own legends and backstory, it may help if the stories predispose them to yearn for each other. Both partners need to be fully aware of the form and attributes of both deities.
- **Each partner steps into one of the godforms and "becomes" the god/dess.**
- **Articles of clothing or other adornment may be chosen as anchors to identify the deities.** These may or may not have some symbolic value relating to the nature of the entities, including colors, symbols, etc. If possible, they should be acquired for and used only for this purpose. These can be put on when the partners step into the entities and worn until the end of the ritual.
- Partners **relate to each other in godforms.** They may speak to each other in the voices of the gods, but will refrain from addressing each other in normal human ways. They will address each

other with the names of the gods, if known, but not their human names. In all ways partners relate to each other as god/desses.

- Within the ritual space, partners **spend some time engaging in shared activities**. Possibilities include eating together, dancing together, chanting together, or playing music together (always as the deities). Activities can be chosen that are specific to the entities, if possible.
- Always maintaining awareness of each other as deities, partners may **begin foreplay**.
- When both are fully aroused, they may **begin a sexual act that will eventually lead to orgasms**. This may or may not include penetration, at the discretion of the partners—a detail preferably decided in advance. Partners maintain this act for at least half an hour, building intensity and then slowing down again repeatedly. Concentration and devotion to the other as a god/dess is maintained throughout.
- At a given signal, intensity is built to a climax, and **concentration on the godforms is continued during and after orgasm**.
- Partners then **disengage, step out of their godforms and remove any associated adornment or anchors**.
- **Godforms are reabsorbed**.
- **The ritual space is then banished again**.
- Partners then **withdraw from the ritual area** and discuss or contemplate their experiences.

✧✧✧

Our godforms can come closer to the ideal, woohoo-inspiring forms of our Inner Babes by accessing some of the physiological components associated with the mirror neuron system. Humans have any number of social rituals designed to activate mirror neurons and create a sense of rapport. We do these almost automatically, when we greet each other, when we share with each other, and when we make love. The more fully we engage in these rituals, the more we use our mirror neurons to blur the boundaries between ourselves. As you'll find out in the exercise below, you already know these rituals. Here are some ways to increase intensity, duration, and novelty.

Exercise A1.2 Mirror Neuron Warm-ups

- With your partner, **agree on three shared experiences** that are acceptable to both of you. In each of these experiences, you will engage in behavior that naturally puts you into identical kinesthetic experience. For instance, in a handshake both partners feel contact of skin on skin in the same place on the same hand. In making a toast, both partners share the same feeling of a glass in the same hand as they make the same movement and say the same thing. These behaviors may or may not include physical contact. Some general examples are given below; fill in the specifics with your partner. (What kind of handshake? What toast? Etc.):
  - Handshake
  - Toast
  - High five

- Shoulder clasping
- Salute
- Waving hello or goodbye
- Hugging
- Dance steps
- Yoga partner stretch
- "Eskimo nose rubbing"
- Kissing

- **Perform each behavior first at regular speed, then in slow motion,** as slow as you can make it. As you perform the behavior, be aware of matching your partner's physiology as much as possible and making sure that you are moving or touching your partner with exactly the same motion or touch that he or she is using. If your palm is touching his or hers in a handshake, make sure that both of you are using exactly the same amount of skin contact and the exact position of palm.
- **Both partners take a few moments to reflect and discuss their experiences.**[4]

Once you have established a powerful flow of information, both conscious and unconscious, between each other using the natural mechanisms of neurology, you can use that flow to evoke a state entity. This requires a good deal of concentration, but will often begin to feel very easy when a strong state of rapport has been established. The Sex Flow Entity is one of the most woohooful evocation methods outlined in this book.

Exercise A1.3 Sex Flow Entity

- **Partners observe each other carefully and begin to match,** as best as possible, in a comfortable and relaxed manner:
  - **Breathing**—match rate, depth, and part of the lungs being used.
  - **Facial expressions**—match muscle tension or relaxation, mouth position, eye positions and movements, head tilt, and any observable facial movements.
  - **Posture**—match overall position (sitting, standing, etc.), curvature or erectness of spine, and neck and head position relative to spine.
  - **Speech**—match rhythm, tonality, pitch, and volume of speech.
  - **Hands**—match gestures, movements, position, and muscle tension or relaxation.
- While continuing to match as much as possible, **partners begin foreplay, moving slowly, initiating and mirroring movements** as in the Mirror Neuron Warm-ups.

- When both partners are fully aroused and ready for more, they **may move on to the main event,** moving very slowly into an easily maintained face-to-face position of their choice, **continuing to mirror and match** as much as possible.
- Partners match **each other in a slow rhythm** that will allow them to maintain for at least half an hour.
- Continuing movement, **each develops an energy flow** as in previous exercises and accentuates it in whatever way proves to be most enjoyable.
- **Partners explain their flows to each other,** describing size, color, movement, direction, and location. Language may be, of necessity, simplified for this purpose and may be supported with gesture and touch.
- **Partners collaborate on a way to join the energy flows.** This is accomplished by letting one flow into the other so that it becomes one single energy flow moving through both people. Let each individual determine what it looks and feels like when it is inside them; just link the cycle of the flow.
- **Intensify the flow** by breathing more deeply, increasing range or speed of movement, or anything else that adds intensity to the feelings.
- At an agreed-upon signal, partners **externalize the energy flow,** imagining it moving a short distance away.

- Continue movement and deep breathing and **send the feelings, breath, and attention into the externalized state entity.**
- In their own minds, partners **may communicate with the entity,** learning its name, symbols, purpose, and anything else that may be relevant.
- If the partners have a previously agreed upon goal or objective for the operation, both **imagine what the attained goal would look like, feel like, sound like, taste like, and smell like.** As each sensory representation of the goal arises in your mind, send it to the externalized entity. If there is no specific goal for the operation, then continue to communicate and learn from this "third mind" in whatever way the entity chooses.
- **Increase movement, breathing, and rhythm until the operation reaches a climax.** Give as much of the experience of orgasm to the entity, to empower the goal.
- Thank the entity, thank each other, then **each partner reabsorbs as much energy and imagining as they put forth.**
- **Banish** the ritual area.
- **Partners withdraw** from the ritual area and spend a few moments contemplating and discussing their experience.

Some principal variations on the exercise include:

- **Split the state entity in two**, with each half identical to the whole. Partners can carry these with them in their hearts after the ritual as a means of bonding or creating a continued heightened state.
- Use the state entity to **empower an imagined human-figure entity**, as in Instant Empowerment.
- **Maintain the ritual prior to when the state entity is externalized**, accentuating and prolonging the energy flow in your bodies for an indefinite period of time.
- Use the state entity to **empower a sigil**.

appendix two

Drugs

So there we were, bipedal primates wandering the plains. We had all this great neurocircuitry in our brains, but we were only using it to get laid. Let's jump forward to the present day for just a moment. Neuroscientists, Ramachandran among them, have come to believe that there are some people who have not "switched on" their mirror neuron system. These folks are generally categorized as "on the spectrum of autism." Now many of these people function fairly well in society anyway; though they may seem socially awkward, they are able to work, have families, and so on. Genomic research has demonstrated that all of these people, including severely autistic children, have the genes and probably the neural circuitry for a functioning mirror neuron system, however, for reasons unknown, those particular genes are not activated. In a *Scientific American* piece on mirror neurons and autism, Ramachandran suggested that chemical agents might be identified that would switch on the mirror neurons for autistic people. One candidate for a possible mirror neuron-activating drug, he offered, was MDMA, the empathogenic phenethylamine more commonly known as Ecstasy.[1]

I have long been fascinated with the ideas that Terence McKenna put forth in his 1993 book *Food of the Gods*, paramount among them the thought that psilocybin in the diet of early humans was instrumental in the development of language, music, and culture.[2]

> *The primate tendency to form dominance hierarchies was temporarily interrupted for about 100,000 years by the psilocybin in the Paleolithic diet. This behavioral style of male dominance was chemically interrupted by psilocybin in the diet, so it allowed the style of social organization called partnership to emerge, and that occurred during the period when language, altruism, planning, moral values, esthetics, music and so forth—everything associated with humanness—emerged during that period. About 12,000 years ago, the mushrooms left the human diet because they were no longer available due to climatological change and the previous tendency to form dominance hierarchies re-emerged. So, this is what the historic dilemma is: we have all these qualities that were evolved during the suppression of male dominance that are now somewhat at loggerheads with the tendency of society in a situation of re-established male dominance. The Paleolithic situation was orgiastic and this made it impossible for men to trace lines of male paternity, consequently there was no concept of "my children"*

for men. It was "our children" meaning "we, the group." This orgiastic style worked into the effects of higher doses of psilocybin to create a situation of frequent boundary dissolution. That's what sexuality is, on one level, about and it's what psychedelics, on another level, are about. With the termination of this orgiastic, mushroom using style of existence, a very neurotic and repressive social style emerged which is now worldwide and typical of western civilization.—Terence McKenna[3]

It's one of those mentally stimulating speculations that McKenna was so good at producing. Alas, short of a time machine, we have little way to prove his hypothesis. But just imagine if some ritual or chemical circumstances would fire up mirror neurons for a whole protohuman tribe at once. The result would be a big, boundary-dissolving group experience. Hell, it would probably be a big orgy. As I write this piece, brain scan studies involving psilocybin are underway, so we soon may know if McKenna's fungal friends also activate the parts of our brains that allow us to share experience and dissolve the ego boundaries that, in part, define our present culture. I think it's a fair bet, with an additional bonus, perhaps. Recent genomic studies of LSD demonstrate that acid very specifically targets genes involved with neuroplasticity, with the brain's ability to rewire itself and learn on a deep level. I would be surprised if psilocybin didn't also express a similar set of genes. If both these speculations prove true, then we have substances that not only can aid in the dissolution of ego boundaries, but also encode this experience in the brain as a fundamental way of experiencing the world.

Additional evidence that psychedelic drugs can access the mirror neuron system and model-building faculties of the brain comes in the form of, you guessed it, entities. Some, but not all, of these substances can induce states in which users report contact with entities of all different kinds, including the God of monotheistic religions, elves, angels, demons, plant spirits, power animals, the spirits of other humans, and cartoon characters. A particularly well-known phenomenon, for instance, is the experience of "elves" associated with the use of the tryptamine drug DMT.[4]

When we perceive an experience, our minds can be aware of only a limited amount of information. A vast amount of information passes by our conscious minds. Some of this is obvious: there are wavelengths of light and sound that we are unequipped to perceive. There are processes happening on an extremely small level—among molecules, atoms, and subatomic particles—and there are processes happening on a vast scale, including the motion of the planet, sun, solar system, and galaxies. But all of that information—and more—is contained or implied in most experiences. When we change our perceptions using a drug or plant medicine, we change the way our brains process perceptions. Suddenly a different range of information from the same experience can be available to us. Our tendency to recognize entities will find and represent to us the patterns of information that reflect a whole—and we perceive elves, demons, angels, gods, and other imaginary friends of various sorts, who may display a unique type of wisdom.

The psychoactive plants earn human or entity names: cannabis is marijuana, Mary Jane; *Salvia divinorum* is Sally or, in Mazatec lore, the herb of Maria the shepherdess; psilocybin mushrooms are Teonanacatl, flesh of the gods; the mescaline-containing San Pedro cactus is named for Saint Peter; Iboga is the guide to the ancestors;[5] and the powerfully psychoactive Datura plant is called the Devil's Root.

Many of these plants are considered to possess indwelling spirits, an intelligence that seeks to communicate with humans through the psychedelic experience. In our ongoing metaphor of neurological modeling, we can understand these spirits as interactions between the state induced by the medicine and our entity-delineating brain. As we might with any state that we experience, we can access a state entity and derive information from it. The state represents chemical information from the plant and the state entity can communicate that information and a wide variety of related, implied information.

For instance, the cannabis plant contains a rather lengthy list of potentially psychoactive substances called cannabinoids. The two best studied are THC and CBD. THC is more psychedelic and stimulates arousal of the brain and increased awareness, among other things. CBD, on the other hand, tends to slow things down, relax, and send consciousness toward snooze-land. Every cannabis plant has a unique balance of cannabinoids, including a unique ratio of THC to CBD. This balance of chemicals depends on genetics of the plant, growth conditions, timing of the harvest, and many other variables, all of which may be conveyed to a state entity on an unconscious level. That plant-specific information can in turn imply information about trade routes and transportation among humans, about the climate in the part of the world where the plant was grown, about the people who live in that part of the world and tend crops, and more general information about the world in which all of this happens. As the state entity is also based in your brain, it can offer information about the interaction of your consciousness with the world that the plant knows.

Please note: *for the following exercises, it is assumed that you have researched and have knowledge of whatever psychoactive substance you are employing, including proper dosage, method of use, contraindications, effects of the substance, duration of the dose, legal status, and anything else pertinent to the exercise and your general well-being. A good place to research such things is* ***www.erowid.org.***

This next exercise uses simple evocation techniques to help create easy, fluent communication with plant spirits. Maintaining concentration may be more or less difficult in the presence of a plant spirit. Having a visual or physical reminder of the ritual process can be helpful. This can be accomplished by placing a symbol, a notebook for recording results, or even a copy of this book, somewhere that you'll be sure to see it, within the ritual space. Enjoy the woohoo, too!

Exercise A2.1 Contacting the Spirit of a Plant Medicine

- **Banish** your ritual space.
- **Take a dose of the substance,** in whatever way is safest and most effective for you. If the substance is one for which the intensity or specific effects may prevent conscious ritual work, then you can work with the state as it begins, as it wears off, or with a memory of the experience.
- **Pay attention to the way the medicine makes you feel,** inside. There may also be visual, auditory, olfactory, or gustatory perceptions at the same time; for now pay attention to the

feeling. Pay very careful attention to HOW it makes you feel, the structure of the feeling. Where does the feeling start? What kind of feeling is it? Where does it go as it develops? Does it continue to move? Is it static? Follow it through to its peak. Then decide: "If this feeling had a color, what would it be?" Imagine the color (or colors) in your body in exactly the areas where the feeling is experienced. Then imagine that you are taking the colored shape out of your body and flip it around to face you. Place it on the floor outside your circle and breathe deeply, feeding it breath and energy on each exhalation.

- **Keep breathing and feeding it energy** until it transforms. The entity may change size, shape, position, movement, brightness, color, or any other factor. Once it has transformed, imagine you are communicating with it. Ask it what it wants to be called. Ask it what it can teach you that it has never before revealed. Ask it how you can feel really good more often or how you can apply its wisdom in your life. Ask about specific situations in your life that you hope to learn about. Find out whatever you can from it. Thank it for everything.
- **Closing**—Absorb the entity and anything else you may have created in your aura during this operation.
- Repeat **Banishing.**

Again, there are numerous variations. The energy flow can be enjoyed and anchored without externalizing it. The plant spirit state entity can add woohoo to larger entities, charge sigils, or be sent off to accomplish tasks. Similarly, you can explore or include drug states with most of the energy flow and entity-based exercises in this book. Different drugs will combine better with different exercises. Exploring even a small part of this woohooful wonderland of choices should be attempted only with a very hardy constitution and a bold spirit of adventure.

Even small doses of some substances can enhance neuroplasticity in practical and controllable ways. A recent study involving a combination of hypnosis and nitrous oxide demonstrated that a small, steady dose of the anesthetic gas enhanced visualization abilities and increased the suggestibility of the subjects.[6] Increased suggestibility is a concept from the field of hypnosis that essentially means that the subject can remember and follow instructions more easily and may be, in general, more open to learning. This points toward neuroplasticity.

Aleister Crowley suggested that larger, acute doses of nitrous oxide could offer students a taste of the mystical experience, knowledge that would allow them to know when their yoga practice was yielding fruit.[7] This brings us to an exciting area of research. Nitrous oxide is a commonly used anesthetic that works by blocking the neurotransmitter glutamate at receptor sites called NMDA (N-methyl D-aspartate) receptors. Lower doses, as noted, may increase neuroplasticity and learning and larger doses may quiet the "me" spot in the brain in a way that allows for a boundaryless experience—and even higher doses cross the line into unconsciousness, entirely extinguishing the concept of "me" (and most other concepts as well). Along the way, entities and other fun phenomena may be perceived.

Another well-studied drug with a similar biochemical effect as nitrous oxide is the general anesthetic ketamine. The effects of oral, snorted, or injected ketamine last significantly longer than an inhalation of laughing gas, but some of the same odd things occur—and maybe even some odder ones. Higher doses of ketamine seem to reboot the brain in a way that allows for sweeping and lasting change to be experienced. Several studies have now confirmed that severely depressed patients given a single psychedelic dose of the drug will demonstrate marked improvement that lasts for months.[8] Pharmaceutical companies are now scrambling to create versions that can be patented for use as a psychiatric medication.

The "brain reboot" experience is an interesting one from our point of view. Essentially, some aspects of the brain seem to shut down, and then, when the brain starts up again, it goes searching for reality, a seemingly very basic transderivational search that, one by one, restores or replaces some of the basic elements of personal epistemology. That is, what you are thinking about when you come back from the "k-hole" becomes, to a large extent, your reality. This experience can be influenced by the "set and setting," what we refer to as the ritual frame.[9]

If, as I've speculated, transderivational search is an actual delineation of reality or a shift into subtly alternate universes, then NMDA antagonist drugs such as nitrous or ketamine may prove to be powerful tools for both therapeutic and magical purposes. Very high doses of other psychedelics, including LSD and DMT, may also affect the NMDA receptors in a similar way. This experience has been equated with the neurochemical pathway of the Near Death Experience,[10] which also seems to offer a "brain reboot," temporary (but radical) changes in experience of "self," and lasting improvements in mood and epistemology.

Of course, these death/rebirth, self/no-self experiences are well over the line into imprinting and initiation and may be explored in the context of the Initiation Ritual Frame, described in a previous chapter.

appendix three

Rock and Roll

So what kinds of songs did our primordial savannah-wandering ancestors sing while munching shrooms during the orgy at the dawn of time? Until the advent of computers, making music was a skill that required the brain's motor functions. Singing uses movements of the chest, lungs, diaphragm, vocal chords, lips, jaw, and tongue. Drumming requires coordinated hand or foot movements. Guitars, pianos, oboes, kazoos, saxophones, cellos, penny-whistles, and pretty much every other musical instrument similarly use motor functions to communicate experience. That is, our brains control muscles that make sounds which convey, to ourselves and others, emotions and states. Emotions and states are deeply tied to motor neurons associated with posture, gesture, facial expression, and breathing, so we can easily say that music can change our state by influencing our physiology. Are you thinking that we're now well into mirror neuron territory? Recent brain scan studies concur—both playing and listening to music are mediated by the mirror neuron system.[1]

Our lives are filled with rhythms. Hearts beat, lungs expand and contract, we wake and sleep, the planet we live on gives us days and nights, tides, and seasons. Each model within a model, mind within a mind, plays along, catching the tempo, playing counter-rhythms, polyrhythms, in an ongoing gamelan orchestra of life. Music joins in, drums catch the beat, strings and winds vibrate in rhythms so fast they flow into shapes, reflecting the dance of our world and our bodies. Our mirror neurons start to party, and the motor neurons zap along with the rhythms, inducing ideomotor movements: a nodding head, a tapping toe, increased heart rate, changes in posture, or full-tilt boogie-down dancing.

The musicians bathe the audience in vibrations, synchronizing mirror neurons, body movements, and encouraging the formation of a group mind. If the band is wild, rebellious, happy, exuberant, angry, sad, mysterious, or in love, then the audience rides along on waves of wildness, rebelliousness, happiness, exuberance, mystery, or love. If the emotion or state that the song conveys is something the audience already feels or longs for, it resonates, fires off more mirror neurons, and fills the people with woohoo.

And if that's not enough woohoo, people begin to dance with each other, observing and matching each other's movements, further transmitting and intensifying emotions and states. Some of the audience members take drugs that further intensify mirror neuron activation. People meet, dance together, and everyone becomes more and more like each others' Inner Babe. We are reflected in each others' eyes. We find commonality in the movement and the music and the moment. We are all together in a single system and the states and information flow freely.

And suddenly we're back dancing around the fire at the dawn of time. It's the primal human ritual, a means of bonding and sharing information that is built into the very structure of our brains. From a modern perspective, it seems as if the primordial orgy was simply about sex, about reproduction for the survival of the tribe. Perhaps it began that way, and perhaps, as with rock concerts and raves, participants rarely thought beyond the hedonic experience, at least consciously. But the ritual—and raves and rock concerts—was at its best a celebration of the individual among his or her tribe, and an expression of the role of the tribe—and humans—in the greater world. The rituals marked the phases of the moon or the cycles throughout the year and thus synchronized the tribal group mind with the rhythms and music of the Earth, Moon, Sun, and stars.

It's a ritual that we're still wired for, that still has meaning in our neurology and physiology. While these ecstatic tendencies are more often co-opted for commercial purposes, even in the case of an overhyped pop concert sponsored by beverage or junk food manufacturers, the experience still takes participants toward a level of woohoo not found in their daily lives. When we start to deliberately return these tendencies to their mystic roots, we find more and more woohoo, and the means to direct it toward specific ends. Lyrics, lights, images, costumes, and stage craft can support the message of the music, that we are all one, that woohoo is something found in our perception of the world, when we can shut off the nattering neurosis of modern life and simply join with other humans in the most fundamental of human behaviors.

While exploring the exercises in this book, you may have noticed that some of your energy flows and entities were naturally rhythmic in some way. Maybe it was in the way they communicated with you, in fluctuations of light or color, in changes of shape or size, in cycling or pulsing. The Rhythm Wave is, in effect, a way for you dance with your own mind-states.

Exercise A3.1 Rhythm Wave

- **Create an energy flow** for a powerful, pleasurable experience.
- **Notice how the energy flow pulses or cycles, or any other way in which it exhibits rhythm.**
- Begin to sway or **move to the rhythm** of the energy flow.
- **Express the energy flow as a gesture or dance move** and incorporate it into the movement.
- **Clap your hands, sing, or play an instrument** to the rhythm.
- **If others are present, have them clap, play, or dance to the same rhythm.**
- When exhausted or when the feelings seem to have peaked, **return to rest and silence.**
- **Notice any thoughts, epiphanies, states, or other experiences** that result from this exercise, either immediately or later.

✧✧✧

Of course, some of your friends may have a sense of rhythm, too, and dancing with a group takes the ritual much closer to its primal origins. The presence of others, again, helps activate the mirror neuron system, which can reflect the woohoo back and forth between you and your partners. The Group Rhythm Wave is a nice piece to build intensity in many different ritual structures and situations.

Exercise A3.2 Group Rhythm Wave

- In a ritual setting, **create a partner or group energy flow.** This can be created by any of the means previously described, including elements from sex magick, the Group Mind ritual, Group Vortex ritual, or any similar technique.
- **Clap together, play together, move together,** dance together to the rhythm of the energy flow.
- When exhausted or when the experience seems to have peaked, **return to rest and silence.**
- The group takes a few minutes to **discuss the experience.**

The Intense Group Rhythm Wave suggests a few ways to add even more woohoo to the experience.

Exercise A3.3 Intense Group Rhythm Wave

There are many ways to add intensity to the Group Rhythm Wave. A few examples include:

- Adding **intoxicants** or psychedelics.
- Adding **erotic components**, including nudity, physical contact, and foreplay.
- Additional **musicians**—drummers or even a full band can participate on the periphery, matching and carrying the rhythm into full-blown music.
- Additional **invocation**—participants can step into deities who are congruent with the energy flow and ritual. They all may adopt the same entity, or some may take on a male deity and some a female deity, or all may participate as elemental characters, as long as every entity can dance to the same rhythm and energy flow.

Again, the more of these elements we add in, the closer we come to that primal ritual. Indeed, as we start to add in intoxicants, erotic components, musicians, and invocation, we are essentially reconstructing classic pagan and Afro-Caribbean styles of ritual. Rituals of this kind can provide intensity of woohoo that can be remembered for a lifetime.

Glossary

Anchor—The sensory stimuli that prompts the recall of a memory, behavior, or experience.

Conditioning—Learning that can be easily forgotten or changed. Ordinary learning as opposed to imprints.

Consensus—A group decision-making process in which each participant has input and the decision is adjusted, added to, subtracted from, and modified until all concerns are addressed.

Default network—A network of brain systems that link up and process memories when conscious attention is not otherwise directed. These parts of the brain are responsible for daydreaming, spacing out, and transderivational search, among other things.

Embodied metaphor—The tendency to create metaphors in terms of the human body.

Epistemology—The basic set of presuppositions that we use, usually outside of consciousness, to create and navigate our world.

Evocation—The act of moving an idea, state, feeling, quality, or memory into a metaphoric position outside the body.

Ideomotor response (IMR)—Subtle or not-so-subtle movements and changes that our bodies make in response to thoughts, often involuntary and/or outside of awareness.

Imprints—Behaviors that are learned in a very deep, permanent way, upon which our general preferences and direction in life are based.

Initiation—A ritual or rite that marks and/or creates deep neurological change.

Inner Babe—Our internal concept of an ideal partner.

Invocation—The act of drawing an idea, state, feeling, quality, or memory into a metaphoric position within the body.

Magick—A means of first perfecting the self so that the things that one may do will be done with power and effectiveness.

Memetic entity—A consciousness based in information, transmitted or communicated by humans, rather than through genetics or biological reproduction.

Memory reconsolidation—The tendency of the brain to change or re-tag a memory each time it is called up from and replaced to long-term memory.

Meta-Magick—Magick used to understand the processes of magick itself.

Meta-programs—Overarching mental tendencies around which other behaviors may be formed, a concept from NLP.

Mind-state—The totality of experience of consciousness at any given moment or in any particular state.

Mirror neuron—A cell in the brain, usually responsible for motor functions, that also responds when we observe motor functions in others.

Neurogenesis—The ability of the brain to grow new cells.

Neuro-Linguistic Programming (NLP)—The study of the structure of subjective experience; a field of practice developed by Richard Bandler and John Grinder, influenced by the work of Alfred Korzybski, Gregory Bateson, Milton Erickson, Noam Chomsky, and others.

Neuroplasticity—The ability of the brain to change and re-form neural pathways.

Ritual frame—Behaviors and symbols that mark out a period of time and everything within that time as being dedicated to a particular ritual goal.

Science—A method of inquiry that uses experimentation to test hypotheses and form theories.

Self-flex—The ability to identify with "selves" of more variety and scope than the singular "self," and, at will, to suppress the "self" part of the brain to a greater or lesser degree.

State-dependent memory—The tendency of the human mind to sort memory and experience by state, making it easy to recall happy memories when you are happy, sad memories when you are sad, and to forget your car keys when you change state.

State entitiy—A representation or metaphor for an internal state of consciousness, often created by externalizing a feeling or energy flow.

Submodality—The subcategories within in each sense. For instance, visual submodalities may include brightness, color, location, size, and focus; auditory submodalities may include volume, pitch, rhythm, tempo, and so on.

Swish pattern—An NLP anchoring technique that associates a resourceful image of the self with the perceptions related to given situation.

Syncretism—The tendency of religions and entities to adapt to changing circumstances by incorporating elements of other religions and entities.

Theory of mind—The ability of our brains to model and make predictions about the consciousness of others.

Timeline—A (usually) linear symbol of time used to bring states and resources into past memories and future projections.

Transderivational search—The tendency of the mind to quickly sort through a range of options when attempting to make sense of words and other sensory experiences. Transderivational search appears to be mediated by the brain's default network.

Woohoo—The indefinable property that lets our brains represent some experiences as powerful, important, or pleasurable. Woohoo is the subtle difference between ordinary and exciting, the factor that makes just another stranger into your friend, your teacher, or your lover. Woohoo is what turns an activity into a passion; it's what changes noise into song, foot movement into dance, travel into adventure, procreation into eros, and biological processes into a life worth living. Woohoo is the measure of intensity. It's what continues to draw your attention, moment after moment.

NOTES

Chapter One

1. Robert Anton Wilson, *Prometheus Rising* (Las Vegas, NV: New Falcon Publications, 1992).
2. Aleister Crowley, *Magick in Theory and Practice* (London, 1929).
3. Stephen LaBerge, *Exploring the World of Lucid Dreaming*. (New York: Ballantine Books, 1991).
4. Dana R. Carney, et al, "Power Posing: Brief Nonverbal Displays Affect Neuroendocrine Levels and Risk Tolerance" *Psychological Science* 21, no. 10 (September 2010): 1363–68.
5. Philip H. Farber, *The Book of Exhilaration and Mastery* (e-book) (Kingston, New York: Hawk Ridge Productions, 2006).
6. D. Overton, "Major theories of state-dependent learning." In B. Ho et al. *Drug discrimination and state-dependent learning* (New York: Academic Press, 1978).

7. R. Fischer, "A cartography of ecstatic and meditative states." *Science* 174 (1971).

8. Robert Dilts and Judith DeLozier. *Encyclopedia of Systemic Neuro-Linguistic Programming and NLP New Coding* (Scotts Valley, CA: NLP University Press, 2000), 1467.

Chapter Two

1. Richard Bandler and Will MacDonald. *An Insider's Guide to Sub-Modalities* (Capitola, CA: Meta Publications, 1988).

2. Karim Nader and Oliver Hardt, "A single standard for memory: the case for reconsolidation." *Nature Reviews Neuroscience* 10 (March 2009): 224–234.

3. Marcus E. Raichle et al., "A default mode of brain function." *Proceedings of the National Academy of Sciences* 98, no. 2 (January 16, 2001): 676–682.

4. Aleister Crowley, *The Confessions of Aleister Crowley* (New York: Penguin, 1989), 810.

5. Do you really need a citation to know that? Test the idea out in the laboratory of your consciousness.

Chapter Three

1. Aleister Crowley, Ed. *The Goetia of Solomon the King* (Foyers, England: The Society for the Propagation of Religious Truth, 1904. Reprint. New York: Magickal Childe Publications, 1992).

2. S.L. MacGregor Mathers, Trans. The Book of the *Sacred Magic of Abra-Melin, the Mage* (New York: Dover Publications, 1975).

3. Farber, Philip H. *Meta-Magick: The Book of Atem* (San Francisco: Weiser Books, 2008).

4. Milton H. Erickson; Ernest L. Rossi Ed. *The Collected Papers of Milton H. Erickson, III. Perceptual and Psychophysiological Processes* (New York: Irvington, 1980).

5. Vittorio Gallese, et al, "Action Recognition in the Premotor Cortex." *Brain* 119, no. 2 (April 1996).

6. V. S. Ramachandran, *A Brief Tour of Human Consciousness* (Essex, England: Pi Press, 2005).

7. Rizzolatti, Giacomo, et al. "Mirrors in the Mind." *Scientific American,* November 2006.

8. ibid.

9. Farber 2008.

10. Andreas, Connierae and Tamara Andreas. *CORE Transformation: Reaching the Wellspring Within* (Moab, Utah: Real People Press, 1994).

Chapter Four

1. Uddin, Lucina Q., et al. "The self and social cognition: the role of cortical midline structures and mirror neurons." *Trends in Cognitive Science* 11, no. 4 (2007).

2. Adapted from Farber 2006.

Chapter Five

1. Joseph E. LeDoux, *Synaptic self: how our brains become who we are* (New York: Viking, 2002).
2. CD Nichols and E. Sanders-Bush, "A single dose of lysergic acid diethylamide influences gene expression within the mammalian brain." *Neuropsychopharmacology*, 26, no. 5 (2002): 634–42.
3. Santarelli L, Saxe M, Gross C, et al. "Requirement of hippocampal neurogenesis for the behavioral effects of antidepressants". *Science* **301** (5634): 805–9, August 2003.
4. Henriette van Praag, "Neurogenesis and Exercise: Past and Future Directions." *NeuroMolecular Medicine* 10, no. 2, (June 2008): 128–40.
5. Crowley 1929.
6. Richard Davidson and Antoine Lutz, "Buddha's Brain: Neuroplasticity and Meditation," *IEEE Signal Processing Magazine,* January 2008,172–6.
7. Richard Bandler, *Using Your Brain for a Change.* (Moab, Utah: Real People Press, 1985).

Chapter Six

1. Mark Stavish, "Assumption of Godform." *Hermetics Resource Site,* 1998. http://www.hermetics.org/stavish/Godforms.html.
2. Dolores Ashcroft-Nowicki, *The Sacred Cord Meditations* (Wellingborough, Northhamptonshire: Aquarian Press, 1990).

3. Ernest L. Rossi, and Kathryn L. Rossi, "The Neuroscience of Observing Consciousness and Mirror Neurons in Therapeutic Hypnosis." *American Journal of Clinical Hypnosis,* 48, no. 4 (April 2006): 263–78.
4. V. S. Ramachandran, "Brain in a Vat." *Edge,* 2006. http://www.edge.org/3rd_culture/ramachandran06/ramachandran06_index.html.
5. Vittorio Gallese and George Lakoff. "The Brain's Concepts: The Role of the Sensory-Motor System in Conceptual Knowledge." *Cognitive Neuropsychology,* 2005. http://www.unipr.it/arpa/mirror/pubs/pdffiles/Gallese-Lakoff_2005.pdf.

Chapter Seven

1. If you're not familiar with this ritual, that's okay. It is easily found in many books and online. But read on, you'll get the idea.
2. Philip H. Farber, *FutureRitual: Magick for the 21st Century* (Chicago: Eschaton Productions, 1995).
3. Crowley 1929.

Chapter Nine

1. Lynden K. Miles, et al. "Moving Through Time." *Psychological Science,* 2010.
2. Rafael E. Núñeza and Eve Sweetser, "With the Future Behind Them: Convergent Evidence From Aymara Language and Gesture in the Crosslinguistic Comparison of Spatial Construals of Time." *Cognitive Science* 30, (2006).

3. Farber 2008.

4. Steve Andreas and Connierae Andreas. *Change Your Mind and Keep the Change.* (Moab, Utah: Real People Press, 1987).

Chapter Ten

1. Lucina Q. Uddin, et al. "rTMS to the right parietal lobule disrupts self-other discrimination." *Social Cognitive and Affective Neuroscience,* 2006.

Chapter Eleven

1. Konrad Lorenz, *King Solomon's Ring.* (London: Methuen, 1961).

2. Wilson 1992.

3. Nichols 2002.

4. Mircea Eliade, *Rites and Symbols of Initiation.* (New York: Harper and Row, 1958).

5. Wade Davis, *The Serpent and the Rainbow.* (New York: Simon and Schuster, 1985).

6. Fanny Wurm, et al. "Effects of Skilled Forelimb Training on Hippocampal Neurogenesis and Spatial Learning After Focal Cortical Infarcts in the Adult Rat Brain." *Stroke,* 2007.

Chapter Twelve

1. William S. Burroughs and Brion Gysin. *The Third Mind.* (New York: Viking Press, 1978).

2. John Nichols, "Election Matters: Campaigner in Chief." *The Nation,* Nov. 1, 2004.

3. Michael Grunwald, "How Obama is Using the Science of Change." *Time*, April 2, 2009.

4. Wilhelm Reich, *The Mass Psychology of Fascism*. Third Edition. (New York: Farrar, Straus, Giroux, 1980).

5. Farber 2008.

6. C.T. Lawrence Butler and Amy Rothstein. *On Conflict & Consensus: A Handbook on Formal Consensus Decisionmaking*. Third Edition. (Takoma Park, MD: Food Not Bombs Publishing, 2007).

Chapter Thirteen

1. Chuang-Tzu. *The Inner Chapters*. (Indianapolis: Hackett Pub. Co., 2001).

2. Farber 2008.

Appendix One

1. V. S. Ramachandran, "Mirror neurons and imitation learning as the driving force behind 'the great leap forward' in human evolution." *Edge*, 2000. http://www.edge.org/3rd_culture/ramachandran/ramachandran_p1.html.

2. Philip H. Farber, *The Great Purple Hoo-Ha: A Comedy of Perception, Part One*. (Oxford: Mandrake of Oxford, 2010).

3. Paschal Beverly Randolph, *Sexual Magic*. (Magickal Childe Publications, 1988).

4. Adapted from Farber 2008.

Appendix Two

1. V. S. Ramachandran and Lindsay M Oberman, "Broken Mirrors: A Theory of Autism." *Scientific American*, November 2006.
2. Terence McKenna, *Food of the Gods: The Search for the Original Tree of Knowledge.* (New York: Bantam, 1993).
3. Terence McKenna, quoted from "Terence McKenna: Mushrooms, Sex and Society." Interview by Philip H. Farber. *Paradigm Shift*, 1998.
4. Peter Meyer, "Apparent Communication with Discarnate Entities Related to DMT." *Psychedelic Monographs and Essays* 6 (1993).
5. Richard Evans Schultes and Albert Hofmann. *Plants of the Gods.* (Rochester, Vermont: Healing Arts Press, 1992).
6. Matthew Whalley, et al. "Enhancement of suggestibility and imaginative ability with nitrous oxide." *Psychopharmacology*, 2008.
7. Crowley 1929.
8. Bill Deakin, et al. "Glutamate and the Neural Basis of the Subjective Effects of Ketamine." *Archives of General Psychiatry* 65, no. 2 (February 2008).
9. Farber 1995.
10. Jansen, Karl. *Ketamine: Dreams and Realities.* (New York: MAPS, 2004.)

Appendix Three

1. Istvan Molnar-Szakacs and Katie Overy. "Music and Mirror Neurons: From Motion to 'E' Motion." *Social Cognitive and Affective Neuroscience* 1, no. 3 (2006): 235–41.

Bibliography

Andreas, Connierae and Tamara Andreas. *CORE Transformation: Reaching the Wellspring Within.* Moab, UT: Real People Press, 1994.

Andreas, Steve and Connierae Andreas. *Change Your Mind and Keep the Change.* Moab, UT: Real People Press, 1987.

Ashcroft-Nowicki, Dolores. *The Sacred Cord Meditations.* Wellingborough, Northhamptonshire: Aquarian Press, 1990.

Bandler, Richard and Will MacDonald. *An Insider's Guide to Sub-Modalities.* Capitola, CA: Meta Publications, 1988.

Bandler, Richard. *Using Your Brain for a Change.* Moab, UT: Real People Press, 1985.

Butler, C.T. Lawrence and Amy Rothstein. *On Conflict & Consensus: A Handbook on Formal Consensus Decisionmaking.* Third Edition. Takoma Park, MD: Food Not Bombs Publishing, 2007.

Burroughs, William S. and Brion Gysin. *The Third Mind.* New York: Viking Press, 1978.

Carney, Dana R., et al. "Power Posing: Brief Nonverbal Displays Affect Neuroendocrine Levels and Risk Tolerance" *Psychological Science* 21, no. 10 (September 2010):1363–68.

Chuang-Tzu. *The Inner Chapters.* Indianapolis: Hackett Pub. Co., 2001. Farber 2008.

Crowley, Aleister. *The Confessions of Aleister Crowley.* New York: Penguin, 1989, 810.

Crowley, Aleister. ed. *The Goetia of Solomon the King.* Foyers, England: The Society for the Propagation of Religious Truth, 1904. Reprint. New York: Magickal Childe Publications, 1992.

Crowley, Aleister. *Magick in Theory and Practice.* London, 1929.

Davidson, Richard and Antoine Lutz. "Buddha's Brain: Neuroplasticity and Meditation," *IEEE Signal Processing Magazine,* January 2008, 172–6.

Davis, Wade. *The Serpent and the Rainbow.* New York: Simon and Schuster, 1985.

Deakin, Bill, et al. "Glutamate and the Neural Basis of the Subjective Effects of Ketamine." *Archives of General Psychiatry* 65, no. 2 (February 2008).

Dilts, Robert and Judith DeLozier. *Encyclopedia of Systemic Neuro-Linguistic Programming and NLP New Coding.* Scotts Valley, CA: NLP University Press, 2000, 1467.

Eliade, Mircea. *Rites and Symbols of Initiation.* New York: Harper and Row, 1958.

Erickson, Milton H.; Ernest L. Rossi Ed. *The Collected Papers of Milton H. Erickson, III. Perceptual and Psychophysiological Processes.* New York: Irvington, 1980.

Farber, Philip H. *The Book of Exhilaration and Mastery.* (e-book) Kingston, NY: Hawk Ridge Productions, 2006.

Farber, Philip H. *FutureRitual: Magick for the 21st Century.* Chicago: Eschaton Productions, 1995.

Farber, Philip H. *The Great Purple Hoo-Ha: A Comedy of Perception, Part One.* Oxford, England: Mandrake of Oxford, 2010.

Farber, Philip H. *Meta-Magick: The Book of Atem.* San Francisco: Weiser Books, 2008.

Fischer, R. "A cartography of ecstatic and meditative states." *Science,* 174, 1971.

Gallese, Vittorio et al. "Action Recognition in the Premotor Cortex." *Brain,* 119, no. 2 (April 1996).

Gallese, Vittorio and George Lakoff. "The Brain's Concepts: The Role of the Sensory-Motor System in Conceptual Knowledge." *Cognitive Neuropsychology,* 2005. http://www.unipr.it/arpa/mirror/pubs/pdffiles/Gallese-Lakoff_2005.pdf.

Grunwald, Michael. "How Obama is Using the Science of Change." *Time,* April 2, 2009.

Jansen, Karl. *Ketamine: Dreams and Realities.* New York: MAPS, 2004.

LaBerge, Stephen. *Exploring the World of Lucid Dreaming.* New York: Ballantine Books, 1991.

LeDoux, Joseph E. *Synaptic Self: How Our Brains Become Who We Are.* New York: Viking, 2002.

Lorenz, Konrad. *King Solomon's Ring.* London: Methuen, 1961.

Mathers, S.L. MacGregor. Trans. *The Book of the Sacred Magic of Abra-Melin, the Mage.* New York: Dover Publications, 1975.

McKenna, Terence. *Food of the Gods: The Search for the Original Tree of Knowledge.* New York: Bantam, 1993.

McKenna, Terence, quoted from "Terence McKenna: Mushrooms, Sex and Society." Interview by Philip H. Farber. *Paradigm Shift,* 1998.

Meyer, Peter. "Apparent Communication with Discarnate Entities Related to DMT." *Psychedelic Monographs and Essays 6*, 1993.

Miles, Lynden K., et al. "Moving Through Time." *Psychological Science,* 2010.

Molnar-Szakacs, Istvan and Katie Overy. "Music and Mirror Neurons: From Motion to 'E' Motion." *Social Cognitive and Affective Neuroscience* 1(3): 235–241, 2006.

Nader, Karim & Oliver Hardt, "A Single Standard for Memory: The Case for Reconsolidation." *Nature Reviews Neuroscience* 10, 224–234 (March 2009).

Nichols, C. D. and E. Sanders-Bush. "A single dose of lysergic acid diethylamide influences gene expression within the mammalian brain." *Neuropsychopharmacology.* 26, no. 5 (2002): 634–42.

Nichols, John. "Election Matters: Campaigner in Chief." *The Nation,* Nov. 1, 2004.

Núñeza, Rafael E. and Eve Sweetser "With the Future Behind Them: Convergent Evidence From Aymara Language and Gesture in the Crosslinguistic Comparison of Spatial Construals of Time." *Cognitive Science* 30 (2006).

Overton, D. "Major Theories of State-Dependent Learning." In B. Ho et al. *Drug Discrimination and State-Dependent Learning.* New York: Academic Press, 1978.

Raichle, Marcus E., et al., "A Default Mode of Brain Function." *Proceedings of the National Academy of Sciences* 98, no. 2 (January 16, 2001): 676–82.

Ramachandran, V.S. "Brain in a Vat." *Edge,* 2006. http://www.edge.org/3rd_culture/ramachandran06/ramachandran06_index.html.

Ramachandran, V.S. *A Brief Tour of Human Consciousness.* Essex, England: Pi Press, 2005.

Ramachandran, V.S. and Lindsay M Oberman. "Broken Mirrors: A Theory of Autism." *Scientific American,* November 2006.

Ramachandran, V. S. "Mirror Neurons and Imitation Learning as the Driving Force Behind 'The Great Leap Forward' in Human Evolution." *Edge,* 2000. http://www.edge.org/3rd_culture/ramachandran/ramachandran_p1.html.

Randolph, Paschal Beverly. *Sexual Magic.* Magickal Childe Publications, 1988.

Reich, Wilhelm. *The Mass Psychology of Fascism.* Third Edition. New York: Farrar, Straus, Giroux, 1980.

Rizzolatti, Giacomo, et al. "Mirrors in the Mind." *Scientific American,* November 2006.

Rossi, Ernest L. and Kathryn L. Rossi, "The Neuroscience of Observing Consciousness and Mirror Neurons in Therapeutic Hypnosis." *American Journal of Clinical Hypnosis* 48, no. 4 (April 2006): 263–78.

Santarelli L, Saxe M, Gross C, et al. "Requirement of Hippocampal Neurogenesis for the Behavioral Effects of Antidepressants." *Science* 301 (5634): 805–9, August 2003.

Schultes, Richard Evans and Albert Hofmann. *Plants of the Gods*. Rochester, VT: Healing Arts Press, 1992.

Stavish, Mark. "Assumption of Godform." *Hermetics Resource Site*, 1998. http://www.hermetics.org/stavish/Godforms.html.

Uddin, Lucina Q., et al. "rTMS to the Right Parietal Lobule Disrupts Self-Other Discrimination." *Social Cognitive and Affective Neuroscience*, 2006.

Uddin, Lucina Q., et al. "The Self and Social Cognition: The Role of Cortical Midline Structures and Mirror Neurons." *Trends in Cognitive Science* 11, no. 4 (2007).

van Praag, Henriette. "Neurogenesis and Exercise: Past and Future Directions." *NeuroMolecular Medicine* 10, no. 2 (June 2008):128–40.

Wilson, Robert Anton. *Prometheus Rising*. Las Vegas: New Falcon Publications, 1992.

Whalley, Matthew, et al. "Enhancement of Suggestibility and Imaginative Ability with Nitrous Oxide." *Psychopharmacology*, 2008.

Wurm, Fanny, et al. "Effects of Skilled Forelimb Training on Hippocampal Neurogenesis and Spatial Learning After Focal Cortical Infarcts in the Adult Rat Brain." *Stroke*, 2007.

INDEX